To Dean & Dorothy
with Love,
Paula & Al

28 Days to Ecstasy
FOR COUPLES

28 Days to Ecstasy

FOR COUPLES

TANTRA STEP *by* STEP

PALA COPELAND & AL LINK

Llewellyn Publications
Woodbury, Minnesota

First Edition
First Printing, 2007

Book design by Joanna Willis
Cover design by Ellen Dahl
Cover photograph © Image Source/PunchStock
Interior illustrations © Matthew Archambault

Llewellyn is a registered trademark of Llewellyn Worldwide, Ltd.

Library of Congress Cataloging-in-Publication Data
Copeland, Pala.
    28 days to ecstasy for couples: tantra step by step / Pala Copeland and Al Link.—1st ed.
        p.   cm.
    ISBN-13: 978-0-7387-0999-4
    1. Sex. 2. Sex instruction. 3. Sex—Religious aspects—Tantrism. 4. Tantrism. I. Link, Al. II. Title.
    III. Title: Twenty-eight days to ecstasy for couples.
    HQ23.C647 2007
    613.9'6—dc22
                                                                            2007032738

Llewellyn Worldwide does not participate in, endorse, or have any authority or responsibility concerning private business transactions between our authors and the public.

All mail addressed to the author is forwarded but the publisher cannot, unless specifically instructed by the author, give out an address or phone number.

Any Internet references contained in this work are current at publication time, but the publisher cannot guarantee that a specific location will continue to be maintained. Please refer to the publisher's website for links to authors' websites and other sources.

Cover models used for illustrative purposes only and may not endorse or represent the book's subject.

Llewellyn Publications
A Division of Llewellyn Worldwide, Ltd.
2143 Wooddale Drive, Dept. 978-0-7387-0999-4
Woodbury, MN 55125-2989, U.S.A.
www.llewellyn.com

Printed in the United States of America

Contents

ONE **Tantra for You . . . 1**

TWO **How to Use This Book . . . 7**

    THE 28-DAY PLAN . . . 8

    CONTINUING YOUR PRACTICE . . . 10

    NOTES TO ASSIST YOU . . . 10

THREE **The 28-Day Ecstasy Plan . . . 13**

    WEEK 1 . . . 15

      Day 1   16

      Day 2   22

      Day 3   29

      Day 4   33

      Day 5   38

      Day 6   40

      Day 7: Tantra Loving Session One—No-Goal Lovemaking   43

WEEK 2 . . . 51

    Day 8   *52*

    Day 9   *55*

    Day 10   *58*

    Day 11   *60*

    Day 12   *62*

    Day 13   *64*

    Day 14: Tantra Loving Session Two—Introducing Ceremony   *67*

WEEK 3 . . . 73

    Day 15   *74*

    Day 16   *78*

    Day 17   *81*

    Day 18   *83*

    Day 19   *86*

    Day 20   *88*

    Day 21: Tantra Loving Session Three—Moving Energy   *90*

WEEK 4 . . . 99

    Day 22   *100*

    Day 23   *102*

    Day 24   *106*

    Day 25   *108*

    Day 26   *111*

    Day 27   *113*

    Day 28: Tantra Loving Session Four—Lovers' Ritual   *115*

FOUR **Tantric Loving Step by Step** . . . 125

    INTENTION . . . 126

    CREATING A SACRED SPACE . . . 126

    THE LOVERS' PURIFYING BATH . . . 127

    HONOR, RESPECT, AND PERMISSION . . . 127

    TUNING IN TO SEXUAL PLAY . . . 127

    GOING THE DISTANCE . . . 127

    MOVING AND SHARING YOUR ENERGY . . . 128

    AFTERPLAY . . . 128

FIVE **Ecstasy Recipe—Your Joyous Steps to Bliss** . . . 129

    RELATIONSHIP AND COMMUNICATION . . . 130

        1. Giving and Receiving   *130*

        2. Anticipation   *130*

        3. Tender Talk   *131*

    SEXUAL TECHNIQUE AND SKILLS . . . 131

        4. Kama Sutra Sex   *131*

        5. Positions for Building Excitement   *132*

        6. Positions for Emotional Connection   *134*

        7. Baby, You Are Tops!   *134*

        8–15. Slow Move/Don't Move   *134*

        16. To Ejaculate or Not to Ejaculate?   *136*

        17. Erection Signals   *137*

        18. Internal Prostate Massage   *138*

19. *Men—Masturbation for Ejaculation Mastery*   138

20. *Women—Masturbation for Building a Higher Sexual Charge*   139

21. *May I Watch, Please?*   140

22. *Very Personal Pleasure*   140

23. *Women—Relaxing into Pleasure*   140

ENERGY WORK AND MEDITATION . . . 141

24. *Begin at the End*   141

25. *Whole Lotta Shakin' Goin' On*   141

26. *Thymus Tap*   142

27. *Ecstasy Chanting*   143

28. *Monk's Walk*   143

29. *Masculine Yoni, Feminine Lingam*   143

30. *Energy Awakening with Your Lover*   144

SEXUAL PLAY AND FANTASY . . . 146

31. *Lovers' Music*   146

32. *Making Out à la High School*   146

33. *Body Kisses*   146

34. *Poetic Hearts*   146

35. *Spinning Wheels*   146

36. *Dress-ups*   147

37. *Playing on the Wild Side*   147

38. *Doctor Fantasy*   148

39. *Food for God and Goddess*   148

RITUAL AND CEREMONY . . . 148

40. *Tantric Ritual 1: I AM THAT*   *150*

41. *Tantric Ritual 2: Tricapeta (The Three Taps)*   *150*

42. *Tantric Ritual 3: Honoring Yoni and Lingam*   *151*

43. *Tantric Ritual 4: Outer Space/Inner Space*   *151*

44. *Tantric Ritual 5: Holy Water*   *152*

45. *Tantric Ritual 6: Five Offerings*   *152*

46. *Tantric Ritual 7: Yoni and Lingam Puja*   *154*

47. *Tantric Ritual 8: Emptiness Is Fullness, Fullness Is Life*   *155*

48. *Tantric Ritual 9: Ceremony of Surrender*   *155*

49. *Tantric Ritual 10: Grand Ritual of Tantra*   *156*

50. *Sexual Magic*   *158*

SIX **Continuing Your Practice . . . 159**

DAILY . . . 160

WEEKLY . . . 162

MONTHLY . . . 162

ANNUALLY . . . 163

OPTIONAL SELECTIONS . . . 163

Relationship and Communication   *163*

Breathing   *166*

Meditation   *167*

Energy Circulation and Exchange   *169*

Sexual Fitness   *170*

SEVEN **The Essentials, Plus More Positions for Energy Exchange . . . 175**

    THE BARE ESSENTIALS . . . 176

    INTERCOURSE POSITIONS FOR CIRCULATING SEXUAL ENERGY . . . 177

    TEN MORE ENERGY EXCHANGE POSES . . . 179

        1. The Leaning Yab Yum   *179*

        2. The Handholding Position   *180*

        3. Fixing a Nail   *181*

        4. Pressed   *182*

        5. Clasping Sideways   *183*

        6. Belly to Belly (The Seventeenth Manner)   *184*

        7. The Deer   *185*

    CONSCIOUSLY CIRCULATING ENERGY FOR HEALTH AND HEALING . . . 186

        8. Resting the Spirit and Healing Your Sexual Organs   *186*

        9. Strengthening Your Internal Organs   *187*

        10. Pair of Tongs for Increasing Blood Count   *188*

Notes . . . 189

Recommended Reading and Resources . . . 191

ONE

Tantra for You

Tantric sex, the art of sacred loving, elevates your sexuality beyond the physical. This ancient practice of uniting sex and spirit is especially relevant for modern lovers who long for deeper connection and greater pleasure. A life-view that celebrates the joys of the body, Tantra helps you open freely and fully to your partner, sharing your glory and your vulnerability. While you can spend many years exploring Tantra's depths, you can also realize some of its intense benefits in a very short time, which is particularly appealing to lovers caught in the hectic pace of life today. In fact, this book is written especially for lovers who are very busy. It shows you that Tantra is a practical approach to intimacy that can have a profound impact on your life without requiring a great deal of extra time. It will help you understand that life can be very pleasurable indeed, and that's a good thing—good for you and for everyone and everything around you.

This Tantric sex playbook contains a detailed twenty-eight-day plan with step-by-step instructions for simple, fun-to-do activities that will strengthen your relationship and intensify your sexual and spiritual connection. The exercises are quite short—from one to thirty minutes. On average, you'll spend no more than twenty minutes per day on your sacred loving practice—less time than you may spend watching a sitcom or the evening news on TV. Once per week, there are longer lovemaking periods, in which you will reap great delights from the skills you've been learning.

We've endeavored to present the exercises and activities so that it's compellingly easy for you to take action.

- Chapter 2, "How to Use This Book," gives you brief and direct instructions for working through the twenty-eight-day plan.

- Chapter 3, "The 28-Day Ecstasy Plan," contains the step-by-step plan, with specific exercises for each of the twenty-eight days. We teach you how to engage in non-goal-oriented lovemaking. The purpose of Tantric sex is union with the beloved through shared pleasure, *not* the pursuit of orgasm—although you'll certainly experience many of them.

- Chapter 4, "Tantric Loving Step by Step," explains the eight elements an extended Tantric lovemaking session comprises. You learn how to make love for several hours, during which time both lovers can naturally become multiorgasmic.

- Chapter 5, "Ecstasy Recipe—Your Joyous Steps to Bliss," suggests fifty specific activities to engage in during your extended Tantric loving time. This section is a "recipe" for sexual and spiritual ecstasy, independent of how long or short the session may be.

- Chapter 6, "Continuing Your Practice," provides guidelines for carrying on your Tantric practice over the course of your life together.

The techniques you will learn include conscious intention and attention, sexual physical fitness, intimate emotional connection, and energy circulation and exchange between lovers, as well as sexual, ceremonial, and ritual play. Included with each day's activities is an inspiring message—a thought for the day—related to relationships, sexuality, and spirituality. They help you focus on key elements of your relationship, such as profound intimacy, soaring passion, trust, surrender, and the most expansive love imaginable.

This book emphasizes action rather than ideas. It's a companion playbook to our book *Soul Sex: Tantra for Two*, which is much more detailed in its treatment of Tantric concepts and their role in relationships. This book is short and directly to the point: to encourage you to actually add the practices of Tantric sacred sexuality to your active lifestyle. Just reading the book won't help you much. To receive the benefits of Tantra, you must do four things:

- First, act in spite of any residual shame or guilt about sex you may carry from previous experiences and conditioned learning.

- Second, give yourself permission to experience pleasure.

- Third, open your heart to give and receive love—and reopen it each time it closes, again and again.

- Fourth, actually practice the exercises and apply yourself to the activities that we describe.

If you do these four things, then the exercises in the twenty-eight-day plan, although short and simple, will have a cumulative effect and will transform the quality of your relationship. You are not required to give up the way you currently make love, or anything else important to you, including your values and beliefs. But by the end of these twenty-eight days, your life will have changed, in some ways profoundly for the better.

You can have the relationship happiness you've dreamt about. You can experience the most sublime intimate connection emotionally, energetically, and spiritually with your lover. You can have all the great sex you want.

You can give and receive pleasure and love in abundance. You can heal and become whole. You can have it all. The only question for you to answer is this: how good are you willing to have it?

Sex is essential in a fulfilling mate relationship, unless you have consciously chosen to have one that is platonic, that is, more akin to friendship than marriage. In a true marriage based on lifelong commitment, sexual fulfillment and abundance in love and pleasure are inseparable from relationship happiness. And relationship happiness is the surest, quickest, and easiest route to your personal emotional maturity and spiritual awakening.

Sex is good, and pleasure is not only good, it's actually necessary for peak mental and emotional well-being. Sexual fulfillment is good for you personally, and it's good for everyone else around you. Your children, friends, neighbors, and coworkers will benefit from your happiness, vitality, and positive state of mind. You'll also discover that sexual fulfillment and its accompanying high state of physical, emotional, and spiritual well-being make you more productive in your work, more creative in your art, and more excellent in your sport.

Taking time to feed your body with the sensual nutrition of erotic touch, connecting on the most intimate levels with your lover, experiencing beyond any doubt that you are cared for and loved—these make everything else in your life work better. You're not being selfish; you're not robbing other important aspects of your life by taking time to be Tantric lovers. On the contrary: you're choosing to be free, to live your life to the fullest. You're acting to be completely alive and productive.

If you actually do the short, simple exercises in *28 Days to Ecstasy for Couples*, you may begin to experience anew what it felt like when you first fell in love, rekindle the passion in your lovemaking, realize new heights and depths of intimacy with your mate, and experience sexual and spiritual ecstasy—all within twenty-eight days.

By following this simple plan, you will gradually begin to notice many of these benefits:

- greater ability to communicate intimately with each other

- increased comfort with giving and receiving sexual pleasure

- ease in surrendering to your lover and opening your heart

- increased sexual stamina and endurance

- extending lovemaking over hours and experiencing lovemaking as timeless

- successfully delaying ejaculation

- increased awareness of your sexual energy and skill in circulating that energy through your body and exchanging it with your lover

- building high sexual charges and carrying hot sexual energy with relaxed comfort

- enhanced desire for your lover

- increased passion in your lovemaking, your relationship, and your life

- becoming more readily orgasmic, with the potential for multiple orgasms (men and women)

- increased enjoyment of ceremonial and ritual lovemaking practices

- enhanced creativity and imagination in lovemaking and the rest of your life

- improved health and vitality

- feeling better about yourself, each other, and your life together

- expanded sense of well-being, delight, astonishment, and joy
- balanced emotions
- decreased stress, worry, fear, insecurity, and other negative emotions
- return to playfulness and lightness of being
- experiences of mystery, ecstasy, and mystical states

It generally takes three to four weeks to establish a new behavior pattern or new habit. And this simple ecstasy plan is habit-forming. Once you've been through the twenty-eight days, you won't want to turn back. Rather, you'll sail forward on newly discovered wings of love, happiness, and ecstasy. These are your birthright of body, mind, heart, and soul freedom. You need only claim them with action to know this is the truth.

TWO

How to Use This Book

This brief chapter gives you precise directions on the most effective method for working with the exercises presented in this book. Remember, it's also important to trust yourself, so listen to your body and feel free to adapt the exercises to suit you.

Remember also to be light with yourself and each other. You're opening to a profound and joyous connection. Laugh together. Sex is too much fun to take seriously.

Before you begin your practice, read through the book to get an overall sense of what you'll be doing.

The 28-Day Plan

Do the exercises together.

- Work together for four blocks of six days, twenty minutes per day.

- The seventh, fourteenth, twenty-first, and twenty-eighth days are longer lovemaking sessions.

DAILY PRACTICE

- Both partners, read the exercises before you begin.

- Choose one person to guide the day's activities. Try alternating days of leading and following.

- You may want to read the exercises aloud as you do them, especially the first time.

WEEKLY LOVEMAKING SESSIONS

- Divide up the activities. Each of you take responsibility for a certain part.

- Note: These once-weekly guided lovemaking sessions don't preclude you from making love however you want to at any other time!

TIME AND LOCATION

- Practice with your partner in a quiet spot where you won't be disturbed.

- It might help you maintain your daily routine if you do your practice at the same time every day. For instance, this is a great practice for the morning. Just wake up a half hour earlier and start your day together this way. Your whole day will be charged with love and connection.

- Try to come to your practice rested—you'll get more out of it.

- Sometimes do the exercises naked. It's fun and inspiring.

TIMING YOUR PRACTICE

- Daily exercises are set up to take about twenty minutes to read and complete.

Some people may finish sooner, and others will take longer. Find your own rhythm—it's the right one.

- Each exercise has been assigned an approximate time frame. You might find it helpful to have a watch or clock to refer to, but don't worry about matching the exact time we've given. As you go through your practice, you'll develop a natural awareness and flow. On the other hand, if you're someone who gets caught up in thinking a lot or needs a certain amount of control, using a timer to let you know when so many minutes have passed can make it much easier for you to concentrate on the exercise itself instead of how long it's taking.

IF YOU MISS A DAY

The program is designed for twenty-eight consecutive days, but that might not be possible for everyone.

- If you are together but
  - miss one day's practice, resume where you left off;

- miss more than one day's practice, go back and repeat the last day you did together.
- If you are apart from each other for a few days during the program,
  - each of you repeats, on your own, the exercises from the last day you were together;
  - you can also experiment with some of the exercises from chapter 6, "Continuing Your Practice";
  - when you're back together, move on to the next day in the sequence.

Continuing Your Practice

After you've completed the twenty-eight-day plan, you'll feel such closeness and see such changes in your sexual, spiritual, and emotional connection that you'll want to continue building on what you've learned and experienced.

Try to maintain a daily practice—together and on your own. Even a few minutes per day will keep your juices flowing. We've provided you with lots of practical suggestions. Mix and match activities from the twenty-eight-day plan with exercises from the chapters that follow it.

Notes to Assist You

- *The most important thing about this practice: it's a time for you to connect daily with each other on an emotional and energetic level.*

- The more you can let yourself participate without judging yourself or your partner, the more you'll get out of each exercise. Step outside the world of the mind. Be present in your body. Allow yourself to feel everything. Do all the practices and spend time thinking about them afterward.

- Be playful and light with your practice. Trying to make everything "perfect" will result in undue stress, and you won't be as inspired to carry on. Congratulate yourself for what you do accomplish rather than getting down on yourself for what you haven't yet. We lay out clear instructions, but things won't always go the way we suggest—be gentle with yourself. Take a deep breath and give yourself a mental hug if you feel overwhelmed at any time.

- Let the person who is leading the day's activities lead the day's activities. Even if you are absolutely positive and certain they've left out something or gotten it slightly wrong, surrender to their lead. This is about connection, not control.

• This is a special practice time, not a place to get into your issues. It's a time for learning and growing as cooperative lovers. Set aside your differences and difficulties and come back to them later if you need to address them.

• The exercises are explained for heterosexual couples. Same-sex couples can easily adapt them by simply changing "man" and "woman" to "partner A" and "partner B." Disregard specific instructions for the yoni if you both are men or the lingam if you both are women.

THREE

The 28-Day Ecstasy Plan

WEEK 1

1	2	3	4	5	6	7
8	9	10	11	12	13	14
15	16	17	18	19	20	21
22	23	24	25	26	27	28

In this first week of practice, you'll learn the basic components of Tantric lovemaking skills: relaxation, focus, conscious breath, PC pumping, and loving connection.

- Read through the full day's practice before you begin.
- Choose which partner will be today's guide.
- Time required for reading the exercises and practicing them: twenty minutes

Grounding

Over the next twenty-eight days, you'll be learning to work with your sexual energy. In order to do that, it's very helpful to be in a relaxed state in which you feel comfortable, safe, and focused. Grounding is a simple and quick way to become calm, centered, and present. Your intention while grounding is to release tension, blockages, and negative energies from your system. You will replace them with Mother Earth energy—strong, serene, and full of sensual vitality.

As you begin, it's important to remember that, for some people, "energy" can be very subtle. You may not notice anything happening internally when you first try techniques like grounding. Visualizing and sensing energy flow might seem elusive and difficult. If that's the case for you, know that your intention is

what's most important. Your energy will go where your intention directs it, whether you can consciously feel it right away or not.

Time: five minutes

1. Sit comfortably with your feet flat on the floor, your back straight but not rigid, and your hands in your lap or on your thighs.

2. Close your eyes.

3. Take a big breath in and then let it out. Repeat.

4. Relax your shoulders and belly.

5. Focus your attention on your lower belly and your genitals.

6. When your concentration on these parts of your body is strong, begin to imagine a connection extending from your genitals down into the earth.

7. This connection can take the form of any image that naturally occurs to you or that you consciously choose. For example, it could be a tree trunk, a waterfall, an extension of your flesh, or a hollow tube.

8. Picture that image stretching down from your body through the chair you're sitting on, through the floor beneath you, down through the ground below the building you're in, down through the rock, through the bedrock, and through the earth's crust,

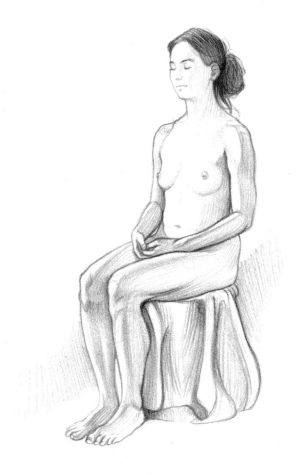

going all the way to the molten core at the center of the earth. Some people may feel or hear their connection to the earth's core rather than see it—whatever your experience is, it's the right one.

9. When you have your connection clearly formed, allow any overwhelming sensations, any negative energies, to leave your body through your lower belly and genitals through your connecting bridge and go down to the earth's core.

10. Consciously release any anxiety, mental distraction, physical discomfort, fear, tiredness, doubt, judgment, or overexcitement. Whatever you do not want in your system, allow it to flow down through your body and empty out through your connection, like sand in an hourglass or water down a drain.

11. When those unwanted sensations reach the earth's core, they are transformed in that fiery blast. They return to you as Mother Earth energy. This energy rises up through your connection and brings with it calm, strength, and sensual vitality.

12. Continue directing negative energies to flow down and away. Allow liveliness, serenity, and power to rise up into you.

13. To help you return to this grounded state more easily next time, use a process called *anchoring*. Touch a spot on your body that is easy to reach and easy to remember. "Anchor" this grounded state to that spot. Later, as you focus on grounding, touching that spot will help you return quickly to the grounded state.

14. Open your eyes and prepare for your commitment ceremony.

Commitment Ceremony

Give yourself a powerful edge by beginning your twenty-eight days with a brief commitment ceremony. Whenever you begin a new undertaking, making a specific commitment to it aligns your desire, your will, and your mental focus. It brings into play your subconscious as well as your conscious mind, so that you have more resources to draw on and a greater likelihood of success.

Time: four minutes

1. Take a moment to silently reflect on the exciting journey you are about to undertake together.

2. When you are ready, open your eyes and stand up. Stand facing each other about eighteen inches apart.

3. Join hands and, taking turns, speak your commitment aloud. Your commitment can be few words or many. What matters is that your words come from your heart—that you speak only what is true for you. Giving voice to your thoughts adds substance and meaning.

Here are some examples to inspire you:

- "[Say your lover's name], I commit to myself and to you to explore Tantric sex over the next twenty-eight days and to be honest, open, and adventurous as we explore together."

- "My love, as we set out on this new path, I commit to practicing with you every day and to be as loving and trusting as I can be."

- "Beloved, I'm so excited to be learning sacred sex with you. You mean so much to me. I promise to do my best in the next four weeks to practice regularly and to have fun with you while we're learning."

4. When you have each made your commitment, continue to hold hands while moving on to the next exercise: looks of love.

Looks of Love

Time: two minutes

1. For one minute, the woman sends her partner looks of love. Making full eye contact, she allows all the tenderness, passion, and affection she feels for her mate to pass through her eyes and into his. No words are spoken and no sounds intrude; only love is passed from eye to eye and soul to soul. He allows himself to receive her love, letting it suffuse him and envelop him without question, without doubt or fear.

2. After one minute, the woman lightly squeezes her partner's hand to let him know it's his turn.

3. He sends his love to her in the same manner—freely given, freely received.

4. When this second minute has passed, he squeezes her hand. Both then say "Thank you" aloud.

Some pointers to help you with the looks of love:

- This is a very powerful connecting exercise. You may find it a little uncomfortable, or even overwhelming at first. You might laugh or want to look away quickly. Persevere. Your nervousness will pass as your hearts open more and more to each other.

- Don't worry about counting out exactly one minute. Simply carry on with your loving look for as long as you comfortably can. At first, one minute may seem like a very long time, but as you progress through your Tantric practice, that will change.

- You may find it easier to focus on one of your partner's eyes rather than trying to look into both. Experiment to see what feels most comfortable for you.

Thought for the Day

Read this aloud:

Couples assume that the relationship itself will carry their commitment for them. They can fall into a trap of automatic behavior—taking each other for granted, allowing passion to die, losing interest in sex, forgetting kindness and respect. It is essential to keep commitment alive by renewing it again and again and re-creating it from a new perspective as the two of you change over time.

Ending Your Practice

Time: one minute

End your first day of Tantra practice together with a full head-to-toe hug and a thank-you to each other and yourself. Congratulations! You've taken your first step on the Tantric path to ecstasy.

- Read through the full day's practice before you begin.

- Choose which partner will be today's guide.

- Time required for reading the exercises and practicing them: twenty minutes

Grounding

Time: three minutes

Begin your second day of Tantric awakening by grounding. It helps you make the transition from your busy life to a quiet time of connection with yourself and your lover. It brings you into the "now" moment.

1. Review the grounding practice described in Day 1.

2. Sit comfortably with your eyes closed, shoulders relaxed, hands in your lap, and feet on the floor.

3. Take two deep breaths.

4. Touch your anchor spot.

5. Visualize the connection forming from your genitals down into the earth.

6. Let any negative energies or overwhelming sensations flow away, going down into the earth's core.

7. Feel the vitality, calm, and strength that flows up into you.

8. Open your eyes and move on to the next exercise: PC pumping.

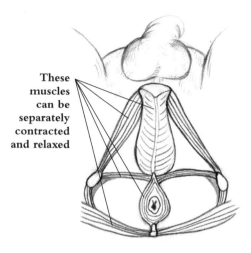

These muscles can be separately contracted and relaxed

MALE

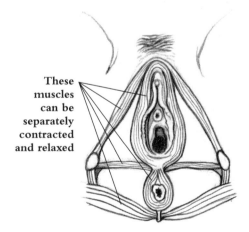

These muscles can be separately contracted and relaxed

FEMALE

PC Pumping

Time: three minutes

One of the most important Tantric exercises is PC pumping, or contracting and relaxing the pubococcygeous (PC) muscles in your genitals. This practice has many benefits:

- increases sensitivity for women, so that their orgasms are easier to have and are more intense

- provides more stamina for men to delay ejaculation and have firmer erections

- prevents or relieves incontinence

- assists in maintaining prostate health

- blocks sexual energy from leaking out of your body and pushes it up through your energy centers

The easiest way to begin learning PC pumping is to pretend that you are trying to stop your flow of urine in midstream or that you have to go to the bathroom but are somewhere you can't. Then, squeeze the muscles you'd use.

1. Sit comfortably and close your eyes.

2. Inhale through your nose at your regular breathing rate.

3. When you've completed your inhale, squeeze your PC muscles.

4. Keep the PC muscles flexed as you exhale through your nose.

5. When you've exhaled completely, relax your PC muscles.

6. Repeat fourteen more times: Inhale. Flex PC muscles. Exhale. Relax PC muscles.

At first, you may find you tighten other muscles as well as your PC muscles—your belly, your shoulders, your jaw. As you gain mastery in this practice, you will eventually be able to keep the rest of your body relaxed while contracting only very specific muscles in your genitals.

Looks of Love

Time: three minutes

Looks of love is such a powerful process that we suggest you make it a daily habit for the rest of your lives. Consciously giving and receiving love energetically has positive effects on your relationship that are not just cumulative but exponential.

1. Review the helpful pointers for doing the looks of love from Day 1.

2. Sit or stand facing each other.

3. Close your eyes and call up the feelings of tenderness and desire you have for your mate. Turn them over in your mind. Feel them in your heart.

4. After a moment, open your eyes and join hands.

5. Today the man sends his love first, allowing his emotion to come unabashedly up and out through his eyes, straight into the eyes and then on to the heart of his mate.

6. After one minute, he squeezes her hand to let her know it's her turn.

7. The woman now radiates her affection, giving her affection permission to well up and out toward her man.

8. He surrenders, allowing her love to penetrate him to his core.

9. When a minute has passed, she squeezes his hand.

10. Thank each other out loud.

Conscious Breath

Time: seven minutes

Breathing with awareness—fully, deeply, consciously—plays an extraordinary role in Tantric loving, as it does in many other spiritual and physical disciplines, from yoga and tai chi to kung fu and singing. Conscious breathing reduces tension, clears your mind, brings you into the moment, heightens your sexual pleasure, and helps you to connect profoundly with your lover.

1. Sit or lie down.

2. Loosen up by flexing and then relaxing all the parts of your body.

3. Start at your feet: tighten, hold, let go.

4. Move to your calves: tighten, hold, let go.

5. Progress in the following order all the way up to your head: knees, thighs, buttocks, lower back, upper back, lower belly, solar plexus, chest, hands, lower arms and elbows, upper arms, shoulders, neck, scalp, face. You may be surprised at how much tension you've been holding throughout your system.

6. When your body is relaxed, begin to focus on your breathing.

7. Place your right hand on your abdomen and your left hand along the bottom of your ribs on your left side.

8. Inhale through your nose, slowly, deeply, and naturally. Feel the air coming in through your nostrils. Follow it all the way down to your belly.

9. Your belly should rise as you begin your inhale. You may even push it out a little to help you relearn to breathe very deeply.

10. Continue to fill your lungs by expanding your rib cage.

11. Feel your ribs moving outward as you inhale. You may even push them out a little to help you.

12. Continue inhaling, filling the upper portion of your lungs.

13. Inhale until your lungs and even your throat, mouth, and nose are full of air.

14. Use a count of four to time your inhale: one thousand and one, one thousand and two, one thousand and three, one thousand and four.

15. As soon as you are full of air, begin to exhale.

16. Do not hold your breath or stop between inhaling and exhaling.

17. Allow a smooth transition from "in" to "out."

18. Exhale slowly through your nose, counting to six. While exhaling, pull in your belly as if you were trying to make your navel touch your spine.

19. Pay attention to the sensation of air as it passes.

20. Inhale again and follow the breath down into your belly, bringing with it vital energy.

21. Exhale and imagine all negativity, illness, and tension leaving your body.

22. Continue to inhale and exhale slowly.

23. If thoughts intrude, gently call your attention back to your breath.

24. Follow each breath, slow and deep, for four minutes.

If you feel a little lightheaded, that's because you're getting more oxygen than you're accustomed to. If so, stop, rest, and breathe as you usually do, then try a few more slow, deep breaths. At first, this pattern of breathing may seem forced and artificial, but before you have completed your twenty-eight-day plan, it will be completely natural. Your body will be very happy to be getting more oxygen—you'll have better circulation and less stress.

Thought for the Day

Read this aloud:

Making love can be an adventure that starts with a jolt of eye contact when you first meet and lasts until your eyes close in death. Be an explorer in the great world of your sexual life. Map the terrain of your bodies; chart the depth of your passion; scale the heights of your intimate connection. Each time you come together, there is always something more to discover.

Ending Your Practice

End your second day of Tantra practice together with a full head-to-toe hug and a thank-you to each other and yourself.

- Read through the full day's practice before you begin.
- Choose which partner will be today's guide.
- Time required for reading the exercises and practicing them: twenty minutes

Grounding

Time: three minutes

1. If necessary, review the complete steps for grounding from Day 1.

2. Sit comfortably, take a deep breath, close your eyes, and relax your body.

3. Touch your anchor and form your connection to the earth.

4. Send negative sensations down and away.

5. Receive serenity and sensual vitality up through your connection.

6. After grounding for three minutes, move directly to conscious breath.

Conscious Breath

Time: five minutes

Today you will be repeating the deep belly-breathing exercise you learned yesterday.

1. If you'd prefer to lie down for this practice rather than sit up as you did while grounding, move into a prone position now.

2. Loosen up by contracting and then releasing all the parts of your body.

3. When your body is relaxed, begin to focus on your breathing.

4. Place your right hand on your abdomen and your left hand along the bottom of your ribs on your left side.

5. Inhale through your nose, bringing air all the way down to your belly, which rises as you breathe slowly and deeply.

6. Continue to fill your lungs by expanding your rib cage.

7. Feel your ribs moving outward as you inhale.

8. Continue inhaling, filling the upper portion of your lungs.

9. Use a slow count of four to time your inhale.

10. As soon as you are full of air, begin to exhale.

11. Do not hold your breath or stop between inhaling and exhaling.

12. Exhale slowly through your nose, counting to six.

13. Pay attention to the sensation of air as it passes.

14. Inhale again and follow the breath down into your belly as it brings you focus and vitality.

15. Exhale and feel any stress or lethargy leaving your body.

16. Continue to inhale and exhale slowly for five minutes.

17. If thoughts intrude, gently call your attention back to your breath.

Looks of Love

Time: two minutes

1. Reread the helpful pointers from Day 1.

2. Today the woman sends first for one minute.

3. The man sends next for one minute.

Endeavor to be fully present in your loving connection. Acknowledge that you are indeed worthy to receive such a genuine outpouring of love, and allow yourself to bask in its glow.

PC Pumping

Time: three minutes

Repeat the PC pumps exactly as on Day 2, but increase the repetitions to twenty-five. As you are contracting your genital muscles, remember to check other parts of your body to see if they have contracted as well. If there are some tight spots, focus on letting them ease into relaxation. Learning to relax most of your body while contracting only a few specific muscles is a key for energy flow during Tantric lovemaking.

1. Sit comfortably and close your eyes.

2. Inhale through your nose.

3. Flex your PC muscles.

4. Keep your PC muscles contracted as you exhale through your nose.

5. When you've exhaled completely, relax your PC muscles.

6. Repeat twenty-four more times: Inhale. Flex PC muscles. Exhale. Relax PC muscles.

Thought for the Day

Read this aloud:

Dare to be vulnerable. Allow at least one other human being to see all of you—your magnificence and your frailty. Gaze into your lover's eyes. Your heart cracks open.

Ending Your Practice

End your third day of Tantra practice together with a full head-to-toe hug and a thank-you to each other and yourself.

- Read through the full day's practice before you begin.

- Choose which partner will be today's guide.

- Time required for reading the exercises and practicing them: twenty minutes

Grounding

Time: three minutes

1. Sit comfortably, close your eyes, breathe deeply, and relax your body.

2. Touch your anchor. Make your connection.

3. Let overwhelming sensations flow down and away.

4. Feel strength, calm, and liveliness flowing up into you.

Conscious Harmonized Breath

Time: six minutes

Expand your breathing practice to include harmonizing your breathing rhythm with your partner's. Breathing in sync with your lover is one of the most profound ways to cultivate your sexual relationship and strengthen your energetic connection.

1. Sit close to and facing each other.

2. Close your eyes. Relax your body.

3. For one minute, breathe deeply and slowly on your own. Inhale, filling the bottom part of your lungs, then the middle part, and finally the upper part.

4. As soon as you feel full of air, begin to slowly exhale.

5. After one minute, place your right hands on each other's chest or belly so you can feel the rise and fall accompanying each breath.

6. Begin to breathe in harmony together.

7. First, the man will set the rhythm, inhaling and exhaling slowly, deeply, and easily in a natural flow. You can use the four-count inhale and the six-count exhale if it's comfortable, but if not, find your own rhythm for full, deep breaths.

8. The woman matches her speed to his.

9. After two minutes, switch the lead so that the woman sets the pace of breath. Arrange a signal beforehand so that you will know when you're switching the lead. A simple signal to let your lover know it's time for her to take the lead can be

to squeeze her hand or lightly touch her shoulder or cheek.

10. Continue, with the woman leading, for another two minutes. Breathe in harmony with each other and with the universe.

You can keep your eyes closed through the exercise or open them—whatever helps you concentrate on matching your breathing. Your focus is to become a natural breathing unit—two lovers, one breath. Be patient with yourself and with each other.

Looks of Love

Time: two minutes

Continue building your intimate energetic connection with unconditional looks of love. Today the man sends his adoration first and the woman joyfully receives it. Then she transmits her affection and he allows his heart to melt under her gaze.

PC Pumping

Time: four minutes

Today you'll add a new component, bringing more awareness and control. It's a gentle "push out" when you're releasing your PC muscles, as if you were trying to thoroughly empty your bladder or get a recalcitrant bowel movement going. Women who've had children will likely be familiar with this bearing-down action (but this version is not nearly so strenuous!).

Begin with twenty repetitions of the "flex and hold" PC pumping you learned on Days 2 and 3, and then move on to add twenty repetitions of "flex and push."

FLEX AND HOLD

1. Inhale.

2. When you've finished inhaling, flex your PC muscles.

3. Keeping your PC muscles contracted, exhale.

4. When you've completed your exhale, relax your PC muscles.

5. Repeat nineteen more times.

FLEX AND PUSH

1. Inhale.

2. When you've finished inhaling, flex your PC muscles.

3. Keeping your PC muscles contracted, exhale.

4. When you've completed your exhale, gently push out with your PC muscles.

5. Repeat nineteen more times.

Thought for the Day

Read this aloud:

Begin to make love instead of just having sex. Open yourself to giving and receiving pleasure rather than trying to perform. Open your heart. Allow yourself to feel emotions as well as physical pleasure. Extended, ecstatic lovemaking requires surrender and vulnerability. Engage in a running experiment to see how deeply you can fall in love with each other.

Ending Your Practice

End your fourth day of Tantra practice together with a full head-to-toe hug and a thank-you to each other and yourself.

- Read through the full day's practice before you begin.

- Choose which partner will be today's guide.

- Time required for reading the exercises and practicing them: twenty minutes

Grounding

Time: three minutes

Repeat the grounding practice. If necessary, refer to the steps on Days 1 and 2 to refresh your memory.

Conscious Harmonized Breath

Time: six minutes

Repeat the exercise for conscious harmonized breathing that you experimented with on Day 4, but this time the woman will set the rhythm first and you will be lying down facing each other rather than sitting up. If necessary, review the full breath exercises from Days 2 and 4.

Here is a concise outline:

1. Lie down facing each other, woman on her right side, man on his left. This pose helps balance masculine and feminine energies.

2. Relax your bodies. Eyes can be closed or open.

3. Breathe slowly and deeply individually for one full minute.

4. Place a hand on your lover's heart, chest, or belly—wherever it's easiest to feel the rise and fall of breath.

5. Harmonize your breathing, inhaling and exhaling at the same time for the next four minutes.

6. The woman sets the rhythm for the first two minutes.

7. The man sets the rhythm for the last two minutes.

Looks of Love

Time: two minutes

Open your hearts to each other yet again. Dare to be transparent. Use the power of your mind to tune out the rest of the world, and focus only on sending your purest emotion to your lover. Today it is ladies first.

PC Pumping

Time: five minutes

Repeat the PC pumping exercises you learned on Days 2 and 4. Today do the following:

- twenty-five repetitions of "flex and hold"
- twenty-five repetitions of "flex and push"

Refer to the full exercise descriptions for review, if necessary. Remember also to pay attention to keeping the rest of your body relaxed.

Thought for the Day

Read this aloud:

As the breath goes, so goes the orgasm: long, slow, complete breath equals long, slow, complete orgasm.

Ending Your Practice

End your fifth day of Tantra practice together with a full head-to-toe hug and a thank-you to each other and yourself.

- Read through the full day's practice before you begin.
- Choose which partner will be today's guide.
- Time required for reading the exercises and practicing them: twenty minutes

Grounding

Time: three minutes

Repeat your grounding process as learned on Days 1 and 2.

Looks of Love

Time: two minutes

Fall into the depths of your lover's gaze. Nothing else exists but the two of you. Men reveal their love first today. Women gratefully receive it and then return the pleasure.

Conscious Circular Breath

Time: six minutes

You'll introduce another variation to your breathing practices today: the circular rhythm. When you become at ease with these breath patterns and add them to your lovemaking, they'll help you circulate and share your sexual energy. If necessary, review the complete descriptions of conscious breath from Days 2 and 4.

1. Sit or lie facing each other.

2. Begin with one minute of deep, relaxing belly breathing on your own to tune you in to yourself and out of the world.

3. Place your hands on each other's hearts.

4. Begin to harmonize your breathing, with the man setting the pace and the woman matching her rhythm to his.

5. Continue to breathe together, inhaling and exhaling at the same time for two minutes.

6. After two minutes, the woman begins to set the rhythm, but this time, instead of inhaling when she inhales, the man waits and inhales when she exhales.

7. Continue this circular rhythm for two minutes. As the woman inhales, the man exhales. As the woman exhales, the man inhales.

What difference did you notice, if any, between the two forms of conscious breathing?

PC Pumping

Time: five minutes

Today you'll add another variation to your pumping routine to bring more dexterity and power. As you're exhaling, instead of keeping your PC muscles flexed, quickly relax and contract them five times in a "fluttering" motion. First repeat the "flex and hold" and "flex and push" pumps from Days 2 and 4.

1. Do twenty repetitions of "flex and hold."

2. Do twenty repetitions of "flex and push."

Now add "fluttering."

FLUTTERING

3. Inhale.

4. Flex your PC muscles.

5. As you exhale, quickly relax and contract your PC muscles five times in a "fluttering" pattern.

6. Repeat fourteen more times.

Thought for the Day

Read this aloud:

Tantra is a form of yoga. *Yoga* means "union." Tantric yoga includes the union of sexuality and spirituality. Sex and spirit are not two separate aspects of our selves. On the contrary, spiritual lovemaking is one of the simplest ways for you to experience a mystical connection—union within yourself, with your partner, and with the Divine.

Ending Your Practice

End your sixth day of Tantra practice together with a full head-to-toe hug and a thank-you to each other and yourself. Tomorrow you go on to your first Tantra loving session!

TANTRA LOVING SESSION ONE

No-Goal Lovemaking

- Read through the entire practice before you begin.

- Time required for reading the exercise and practicing it: one hour

- Additional properties needed:
  - sensual, relaxing music
  - candles, red light bulb (optional)

Most regular lovemaking has a goal: orgasm. If you both come at the same time, you've hit the jackpot; if neither of you come at all, you may as well have spent your time elsewhere. Tantric lovemaking brings a different perspective. There is no goal, but there is a purpose: union with your lover and the Divine through shared pleasure. Such an approach brings less pressure and more freedom. When you let go of the urgency to reach orgasm, you'll likely find you have more of them.

This week you will begin your journey toward "no-goal lovemaking" with an intimate, playful, and pleasurable practice called the "Loving Body Discovery." It is not a massage, nor is it a journey over your partner's body to all the spots—and with all the caresses—that you know will be turn-ons. Rather, it is a very slow, tactile, visual investigation of your mate as if this were the first time you had ever seen each other's bodies, or the last time you ever will. You're not trying to get anywhere. You will give and receive pleasure without aiming for the specific goal of orgasm. In fact, you are encouraged to experiment with *not* having an orgasm, but rather allowing any sexual charge you build to rest within you, without having to do anything with it. Such an approach goes a long way to helping relieve the performance pressure many lovers feel.

You may also be surprised to find that the Loving Body Discovery can be more relaxing and affectionate than sexually stimulating. Whatever happens is right.

Within this allotted hour, you'll have about twenty minutes to explore each partner, but you can certainly extend this time if you wish. It's also an exercise that is great fun to repeat, again and again and . . .

Grounding

Time: three minutes
Let the world drop away so that your focus is here, now, in your body, and on each other. Repeat the grounding practice you learned this week.

Commitment Check

Time: two minutes
Talk to each other about the commitment you made at the beginning of this program. How has it felt to endeavor to live up to it? Has it been easy or difficult for you? Be real with your emotions. Allow yourself to feel everything and explore whatever's there—sadness as well as happiness. Honor each other for reaching this stage in your Tantric sex journey together. Good work!

Looks of Love

Time: two minutes
Ladies first today. Dive into your heart and let your love for your partner swim out through your eyes. Men follow on their sea of emotion.

Loving Body Discovery

Create a sensual ambience for your body discovery:

- Make sure the room is warm.

- Lighting should be bright enough to see clearly but also soft and caressing to your skin—for example, candles or a red light bulb.

- Play music that relaxes you and makes you feel sensual.

MAN—THE EXPLORER

Today the man will first act as the discoverer and the woman the discovered; then you will switch roles.

Begin by asking your lover's permission: "My beloved [or your name for your lover], I come to you with love, desire, and the utmost respect. May I please explore your wonderful body?"

Your lover responds, "Yes, I welcome you with love and trust."

You can make up your own words to show respect, love, trust, and care. Sometimes the receiving partner may be shy or uncomfortable having a particular body segment thoroughly explored. If this is the case, it is important to be open and honest. Tell each other how you feel, and respect your limitations.

1. Start from a distance with a slow, soft, caressing look from head to toe and back again. As you are looking, tell your lover what pleases you about her. Remember, most of us are not accustomed to being gazed at all over, especially with love, adoration, and desire. Your partner may be feeling uncomfortable; ask her to breathe deeply, to relax any tension in her body, and to try to feel the vital energy coming from your eyes into her body.

2. Move closer and mix your looking with touches. Go slowly. Begin with her hands, lifting them, caressing her palms, stroking them lightly, and then gently sucking each finger. Work your way up her arms, feathering lightly with your fingers, repeating the path with a sniffing, tickling nose. Repeat again with pouty, nibbling lips and a darting, slippery tongue. Most women like a gentle touch at first.

3. As you explore, keep letting your lover know how much you are enjoying your

tour. Tell her with words, sounds, and facial gestures.

4. Look into each other's eyes frequently and feel the connection between the two of you deepening.

5. Harmonize your breathing from time to time throughout your discovery.

6. From her arms, move up to her head, neck, and ears, then her eyes, face, mouth, and chin, and finally back down to her neck. Take your time. Feel her skin beneath your hands, smell the unique scent of each part of her, and listen to her breath and to any sounds she may make in response to your touch.

7. Switch from her head to her feet. Play with them as you did with her hands. Then proceed up her legs. Take your time. Be playful. Focus all your attention on your lover and allow your heart to open.

8. When you reach the tops of her legs, roll her onto her stomach and explore her back with your hands, with your nose, with your mouth, and then with a combination of all three, from the base of her neck all the way down to her feet.

9. Once again, roll her onto her back and, starting at the hollow of her neck, work your way down her torso in waves, using your hands, nose, and mouth. Pause at her breasts and belly, or other spots on her torso that give both of you pleasure.

10. Finally, turn your attention to her *yoni,* the Tantric term for a woman's genitals. This is the seat of creation, the wellspring of life. Explore her gently with your fingers, mouth, and nose. Your purpose is to heighten awareness for both of you, not to turn her on (although this may happen). Do not use any habitual touches that you know will bring her to orgasm. If either or both of you become sexually excited, endeavor to relax and *be* with the excitement. Of course, you always have the choice to go on to orgasm, but you're encouraged to experiment with the sensation of high sexual charge.

11. Finish with a complete hug: head to toe for two minutes. Feel your hearts beating. Match your breathing rhythm. In love and respect, thank each other, and then switch partners.

WOMAN—THE DISCOVERER

1. Ask your man's permission to discover his body.

2. Begin with slow, loving looks. Tell him what pleases you about his body. Be bold and reassuring.

3. Very slowly, begin to explore him with touch, working from the outside in: fingers first, then hands, then arms. Use your hands, hair, nose, lips, tongue, and teeth. Vary your touches from very, very light and feathery to firm.

4. Look into his eyes.

5. Match your breathing rhythms.

6. Tell him how much you are enjoying your exploration.

7. From his arms, move to his face, head, and neck, lovingly and playfully. Then go on to his feet and up his legs—slowly, slowly, tasting, smelling, squeezing.

8. Ask him to turn over onto his stomach, and investigate him from top to toe with wonder and delight.

9. Once again, move him onto his back and flow from the hollow of his throat down

over his torso, chest, and belly to his groin. With love and respect and a light heart, make your way to his *lingam*, his penis or "wand of light" in the Tantric perspective. Pay attention to his testes and his perineum—his "p-spot," between the anus and testes. This is a very important part of his sexual body, a part that you'll be coming to know intimately in the weeks ahead.

10. If he becomes highly aroused, ask him to relax and breathe and to simply feel the charge he's been building. It's a great beginning for starting to work with sexual energy. As with the woman, the option for orgasm is of course there . . . but what will happen if he doesn't take it?

Thought for the Day

Read this aloud:

Consider that sex is not just the pleasure of body friction, but is rather primarily an energy exchange. When orgasm changes from something that is strictly genital into something you experience with your whole body, when you can experience orgasm through your toes or your shoulders as well as through your penis, when you are being wracked with orgasmic waves and can't tell whose orgasm it is, yours or your partner's, then you know that sex isn't going to become boring. This is masterful sexual loving. It requires a combination of time, attention, and adventure that you practice throughout a lifetime together.

Ending Your Practice

Finish with a complete hug—head to toe for two minutes. Feel your hearts beating. Match your breathing rhythms. In love and respect, thank each other.

If you have time, talk to each other about your experience. How did you feel discovering and being discovered? What did you like about the practice? Was there anything that you didn't like?

The Loving Body Discovery is a practice you can repeat many times. If you're truly in the moment, it will be completely different every time.

WEEK 2

8	9	10	11	12	13	14
15	16	17	18	19	20	21
22	23	24	25	26	27	28

In Week 2, you'll build on and refine the basic skills you learned last week. You'll also focus on becoming more fully aware of your body and its responses, particularly through your sense of touch.

- Read through the full day's practice before you begin.

- Choose which partner will be today's guide.

- Time required for reading the exercises and practicing them: twenty minutes

Body Scan

Time: four minutes

You've been learning about tuning in to your body during your conscious breathing practice, by first contracting and then relaxing different muscle groups. Now, with the body scan, you simply put your attention into different parts of your organism. Body scanning tells you if you're holding tension—physical, mental, emotional, or energetic—in any part of your body. When you're finished your scan, use grounding to let any tension go.

1. Sit comfortably, close your eyes, and take one deep breath.

2. Focusing intently and noticing any sensations, move slowly through your body as indicated below. At first, it may help you to say each part aloud:

    left foot

    left leg

    right foot

    right leg

    pelvis

    lower back

    upper back

    belly

    solar plexus/upper abdomen

    chest

    left hand

    left arm

    right hand

    right arm

shoulders

neck and throat

head

3. Move directly into grounding after you've completed your scan.

Grounding

Time: three minutes

Repeat grounding as learned on Days 1 and 2.

Looks of Love

Time: two minutes

Men open their hearts first today. Women respond.

PC Pumping and Breath Combination

Time: eight minutes

Today you will combine relaxed, conscious breath with rhythmic PC squeezes. You will learn to contract and relax your PC muscles while you breathe in a slow, deep flow. *Do not match your PC pumping to your breathing pattern. Flex and relax your PC muscles independently from inhaling and exhaling.*

For PC pumps, do the following:

- twenty "flex and hold"

- twenty "flex and push"

- fifteen groups of five "flutterings"

1. Sit comfortably.

2. For two minutes, breathe fully and deeply.

3. Continue to breathe in this slow, deep fashion as you add your rhythmic PC squeezes.

4. Continue your breathing until you have completed fifty-five squeezes—two sets of twenty and one set of fifteen. Do not rush your squeezes. Endeavor to maintain them at the same speed you used last week, even though you are breathing at a different rhythm.

At first, you might find it difficult to make this change. Simply acknowledge it, without judgment or frustration, and bring yourself back to continuous breath. Give yourself a mental hug of encouragement. You're learning the very important Tantric skill of keeping your body relaxed and your breath even while you contract a specific muscle group.

Thought for the Day

Read this aloud:

It's difficult to be fully present in every moment. Your mind wants to distract you with thoughts of the future and of the past, of possibilities and interpretations. Your body knows what is real, what is now. Listening to your body will help you be truly present, not just during your Tantric practice or during your lovemaking, but at other times too. Try it for even one minute per hour daily, and notice the difference it makes.

Ending Your Practice

End your eighth day of Tantra practice together with a full head-to-toe hug and a thank-you to each other and yourself.

Preparation for Tantra Loving Session Two

Your next Tantra loving session, on Day 14, is "Introducing Ceremony," in which you will transform your regular lovemaking space into a sacred space. You'll need certain supplies, so if you start gathering them over the course of this week, you'll have them ready for Day 14. Here's a list of items. It isn't necessary to obtain every single one. You will want to be creative and spontaneous in your ceremony, not rigid. Gather what appeals to you and what you can easily lay your hands on. Have fun.

- candles
- fresh flowers or plants
- large pieces of soft, lightweight colored cloth—such as remnant ends from fabric stores, sarongs, bedsheets, or duvet covers
- incense, sweet grass, or essential oils in diffusers
- ceremonial sound makers: a drum, a rattle, a Tibetan singing bowl, chimes, cymbals
- sensual, romantic, or spiritual music
- bath oils, bubbles, or gels

- Read through the full day's practice before you begin.

- Choose which partner will be today's guide.

- Time required for reading the exercises and practicing them: twenty minutes

- Additional properties needed: massage oil, pillows, towel

Body Scan and Grounding

Time: four minutes

1. Sit comfortably, close your eyes, and take one deep breath.

2. For two minutes, scan through your body from feet to head, as you did in yesterday's practice.

3. Ground for two minutes.

Looks of Love

Time: two minutes
Men send their feelings first, women second.

PC Pumping and Breath Combination

Time: six minutes

1. Take three full, deep breaths.

2. Begin PC pumping as you continue your breathing.

3. Do a total of fifty-five PC squeezes: twenty each of "flex and hold" and "flex and push" and fifteen groups of five "flutterings." If necessary, reread yesterday's instructions.

Foot Massage for Her

Time: five minutes

Although you might think of massage as a whole-body affair that takes a while, you can derive great benefits with just a few minutes of attention to specific body parts. Your hands and feet are mirrors of your entire organism; massaging them can make you feel good all over.

1. The woman stretches out on a bed or sofa, comfortably supported by pillows.

2. You cradle her foot in your lap, with a towel covering you to absorb oils.

3. Put oil on your hands and rub them together briskly to warm them.

4. Take one foot in your hands and, with your thumbs, firmly stroke along the top of

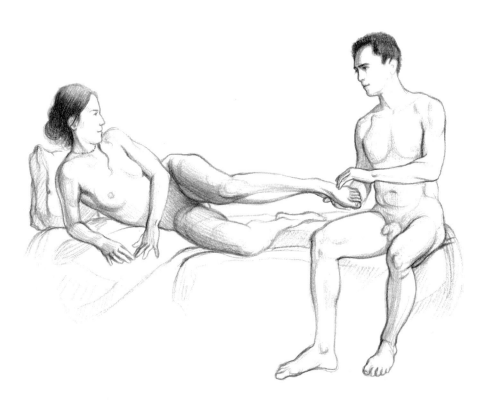

the foot, from her toes to her ankle. Slide your thumbs back from ankle to toes with a lighter touch. Repeat three times on the top of her foot. Ask to make sure you're using a pressure she enjoys.

5. Do four of these same strokes with your thumbs on the bottom of her foot—from toes to heel and back again.

6. Cup her heel in one hand and hold the ball of her foot in the other. Very gently and slowly, rotate her ankle two times to the left and two times to the right.

7. Holding her foot in one hand, use the other to stretch her toes. One by one, grasp each toe between your thumb and forefinger and, sliding down its length, gently pull. Repeat, but this time rub the toe between your thumb and finger as you pull. When you've stretched and rubbed each toe, slide your index finger between it and the next one, wiggling your finger a little as you do. Finally, make circles with your fingertips on the end of each toe.

8. Finish this foot with firm finger strokes on the top and sole of her foot—twice from toes to ankle, and twice from toes to heel.

9. Repeat these steps on her other foot.

Thought for the Day

Read this aloud:

In sacred sex lovemaking, you pass the lead back and forth between you. Both partners learn the unique joys of giving and receiving, of consciously taking active and receptive roles.

Ending Your Practice

End your ninth day of Tantra practice together with a full head-to-toe hug and a thank-you to each other and yourself.

- Read through the full day's practice before you begin.
- Choose which partner will be today's guide.
- Time required for reading the exercises and practicing them: twenty minutes
- Additional properties needed: massage oil, pillows, towel

Body Scan and Grounding

Time: four minutes

1. Body scan for one minute. Endeavor to make your scan faster today.

2. Ground for three minutes.

Looks of Love

Time: two minutes
The woman lets her love out first. He joyfully receives and reciprocates.

PC Pumping and Harmonized Breath Combination

Time: six minutes
Today you will combine PC squeezes with harmonized breathing with your partner.

1. Sit or lie comfortably, facing each other.

2. The woman sets the breathing rhythm.

3. The man follows her, matching inhale for inhale and exhale for exhale.

4. After five breaths together, each of you begins your PC pumps. Do fifty-five: two sets of twenty and one set of fifteen. Endeavor to stay in breathing rhythm with your partner as you squeeze. Your squeezes don't have to match—just your breath.

Foot Massage For Him

Time: five minutes

Today, she gives the foot massage. Repeat yesterday's steps.

Thought for the Day

Read this aloud:

Know your body as a divine temple of love, carrier of the soul, manifestation of God and Goddess. Become truly at home in your body—at ease, at peace, and comfortable in your own skin.

Ending Your Practice

End your tenth day of Tantra practice together with a full head-to-toe hug and a thank-you to each other and yourself.

- Read through the full day's practice before you begin.

- Choose which partner will be today's guide.

- Time required for reading the exercises and practicing them: twenty minutes

- Additional properties needed: massage oil

Body Scan and Grounding

Time: four minutes

1. Body scan for one minute.

2. Ground for three minutes.

Looks of Love

Time: two minutes
Ladies first, gentlemen second.

PC Pumping and Harmonized Breath Combination

Time: six minutes
Repeat yesterday's harmonized breathing with your partner as you do fifty-five rhythmic PC pumps. Today, the man sets the rhythm. Remember, try to stay in breathing rhythm with your lover as you do your squeezes on your own.

Back Rub for Him

Time: five minutes

1. The man lies on his stomach. If he is usually clothed during practice, he has removed his shirt so that he's naked from the waist up.

2. You straddle his hips, facing toward his head.

3. Pour a little massage oil into your hands and warm it by rubbing your palms briskly together.

4. Start at his pelvis and, with the heels of your palms, stroke slowly and firmly up his back on each side of his spine. Men generally like a lot of pressure, so lean into your stroke with the weight of your body. Ask him how much pressure he wants.

5. At his shoulders, turn your hands so that your fingers are pointing out toward his arms. Glide your hands back down toward his pelvis.

6. Repeat nine more times.

7. Starting at the base, make circles with your thumbs all the way up either side of his spine. Continue all the way up his neck to the base of his skull.

8. Massage along the tops of his shoulders, from the neck outward, applying deep pressure from your thumbs or fingers.

9. Repeat five times: up the spine to the neck and then out along the shoulders.

10. Finish with three more of the broad strokes you did at the beginning.

Thought for the Day

Read this aloud:

Massage is relaxing, healing, and sensual. It reduces stress, increases circulation, loosens muscles, and keeps skin supple—a splendid gift to give each other.

Ending Your Practice

End your eleventh day of Tantra practice together with a full head-to-toe hug and a thank-you to each other and yourself.

- Read through the full day's practice before you begin.

- Choose which partner will be today's guide.

- Time required for reading the exercises and practicing them: twenty minutes

- Additional properties needed: massage oil

Body Scan and Grounding

Time: four minutes

1. Body scan for one minute.

2. Ground for three minutes.

Looks of Love

Time: two minutes
He leads the loving gazes, and she follows.

PC Pumping and Circular Breath Combination

Time: seven minutes
You'll breathe in rhythm with your partner while you do your fifty-five PC pumps. This time, however, you will use the circular breathing pattern.

1. Sit or lie facing each other.

2. Relax your body.

3. The woman sets the rhythm. She inhales and he exhales.

4. She exhales and he inhales.

5. After five breaths together, begin your PC pumps. Endeavor to stay in breathing rhythm together. If you lose your way, don't worry. Just ease yourself back in.

Back Rub for Her

Time: five minutes

Repeat yesterday's practice, with her on the receiving end. Women generally like less pressure than men during massage, so be sure to ask.

Thought for the Day

Read this aloud:

Despite popular belief, it is not your lover's job to bring you to sexual ecstasy. No matter how attentive or skillful your lover may be, it's only by allowing yourself to open fully to sexual pleasure that you'll reach the heights of orgasmic bliss.

Ending Your Practice

End your twelfth day of Tantra practice together with a full head-to-toe hug and a thank-you to each other and yourself.

- Read through the full day's practice before you begin.

- Choose which partner will be today's guide.

- Time required for reading the exercises and practicing them: twenty minutes

Body Scan and Grounding

Time: four minutes

1. Body scan for one minute.

2. Ground for three minutes.

Looks of Love

Time: two minutes
She leads the way to love today. He follows with joy.

PC Pumping and Circular Breath Combination

Time: six minutes
Repeat yesterday's circular breathing together with fifty-five PC pumps. Today, the man leads.

Tender Touching

Time: six minutes
Today you'll deliver exquisitely tender touches to neck, ears, and face. You'll use your fingers, breath, and lips.

1. The man goes first. Explore your lover's face slowly and tentatively, with just the tips of your fingers. Make your touch as soft as a butterfly's wing. Trace the curve of her jaw, the line of her cheek, the curl of her lips, and the arch of her brow.

2. Then trail your fingers lightly down to the hollow of her throat and along the sides of her neck to her ears.

3. With the pads of your fingers, massage her ears from the lobe up and then back down.

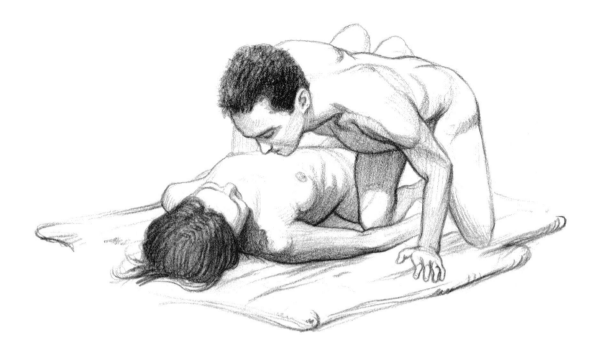

4. Bring your mouth close to her ear. Softly breathe her name and a word or two of endearment, such as "I love you so completely" or "You're the most amazing woman" or "I love to touch you and to please you." Give your loving words to one ear and then the other.

5. With slightly parted lips, delicately kiss your way from her ears down her neck and around to the hollow of her throat.

6. Cupping her face lovingly in your hands, slowly, slowly, slowly and gently kiss her forehead, her eyes, and finally her mouth.

7. Switch roles. Now it's her turn to shower you with affection. Follow the same steps.

Thought for the Day

Read this aloud:

Just as bodies crave dietary nutrition from food, so do they ache for sensual nutrition: the life-enhancing and health-promoting properties of touching. Sensual stimulation, especially caresses, hugs, and kisses, sends a chain reaction of chemicals to signal your brain that this is pleasurable, nurturing, and good.

Ending Your Practice

End your thirteenth day of Tantra practice together with a full head-to-toe hug and a thank-you to each other and yourself. Tomorrow is your second playday; there are wonderful things in store for you both.

TANTRA LOVING SESSION TWO

Introducing Ceremony

- Read through the entire practice before you begin.

- Time required for reading the exercises and practicing them: two hours

- Additional properties needed: see the list provided on Day 7

Tantric lovemaking includes ceremony and ritual to help you remember that this is sex that's more than physical. Ritual reaches deep inside you, to the realm of spirit. It helps you open to the divine mystery of life. If at first you're a little shy or apprehensive about participating in ceremonies connected to lovemaking, remember that you're on a learning journey. Set aside your mental qualms and act to support your learning. Let yourself have fun with it too.

Body Scan and Grounding

Time: four minutes

1. Body scan for one minute.

2. Ground for three minutes.

Commitment Check

Time: two minutes

Talk to each other about the commitment you made at the beginning of this program. Has it been difficult or easy for you to keep it? Praise each other for the efforts you've made to reach this halfway point in the ecstasy plan. You're amazing!

Looks of Love
Time: two minutes
He melts her first with his loving gaze. She jumps in with joy.

Creating Your Sacred Space
Time: twenty-five minutes
You can transform any space you've chosen for lovemaking into a sacred space—your bedroom, the den, a tent, a hotel room. All that's needed is your intention and a few items to add beauty and sensuality.

1. With your thoughts focused on creating a special, sensual atmosphere for your loving playtime, decorate your space with the items you've gathered over the week. Take your time. Be mindful as you light each candle or as you place a vase of flowers on the bedside table. You're setting the scene for spectacular loving.

2. When you have your room set up the way you like, it's time to sanctify it with ceremony. One of the simplest, most elegant, and most powerful ceremonies is this:

    a. Walk around your space three times in a counterclockwise direction

    b. As you walk, say aloud anything you don't want within you or your room. For instance, say, "Out with fear" or "Away with separation" or "I banish judgment and holding myself back." Speaking out loud gives your words more power than if you only think them.

    c. Now walk three times around your space in a clockwise direction, saying aloud all that you would like to invite into your space: "In with passion" or "I invite mystery and wonder" or "In with union, in with love, in with sexual delight," and so on.

    d. You can add to your ceremony with sound makers like drums and bells. You can purify your space with incense, sweet grass, or cedar.

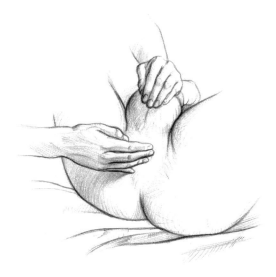

Blessed Bathing

Time: twenty-five minutes

Now that your hearts are open and your room is ready, it's time to prepare your body. Bathing is a sacred ritual in many cultures, and it plays a special part in your lovemaking.

- Bathe together, in a tub if possible, with candles and bubbles or oils. If you don't have a tub, shower together. Wash each other's bodies and hair. Be sexy, sensual, and loving.

- Wash away not just physical grime, but psychic and energetic dirt—anything that

holds you back from loving yourself and your partner completely.

- When you've finished bathing, dry each other with tenderness and delight. Apply lotion or scent to each other's bodies. Prepare yourself for more pleasures to come.

Perineum Massage

Time: three minutes

At some point during your time together—after your bath, after your kissing, during active lovemaking, or between bouts of intercourse—

the woman will give her partner a brief perineum massage. It helps keep his prostate gland relaxed and moves his hot sexual energy away from his genitals, so he'll last longer.

- He lies on his back, with his thighs parted. A pillow under his hips will tilt his pelvis up so that you have better access.

- Pressing firmly on his perineum with your fingertips, massage in circular motions, first in one direction and then the other. You can use oil or lubricant if you like, but it isn't necessary.

The Invitation

Time: three minutes

Reinforce the ceremonial nature of your loving by inviting your partner to partake in this time of pleasure with you.

1. After your bath, return to your sacred room.

2. You can put on robes or remain naked.

3. Today, the man will invite his lover to join him in celebrating your love through your sexual union. Your exact words aren't im-

portant; your heartfelt intention is. Here are some brief examples to stimulate your own invitation.

- "My beautiful goddess, I'd like to show you just how special you are to me, how much I adore you and desire you. Will you be my lover?"

- "I'm aching to touch you, to hold you, to make love to you. Will you celebrate our love with me?"

- "You're so amazing and sexy. I love you like crazy. May I show you how much you mean to me? Will you make love with me?"

Kissing

Time: fifteen minutes

Remember when you could "neck" for hours? Build your desire and your sexual charge really high with fifteen minutes of passionate kissing. You can stroke hair, arms, backs, and shoulders. You can nibble ears and suck on necks, but keep your hands and mouths away from the hot zones of breasts and genitals.

Lovemaking—
Manual, Oral, Intercourse

Time: thirty minutes

After kissing, move on to pleasure each other however you like: manually, orally, or through intercourse. Often, intercourse signals the beginning of the end. The lovers continue until the man ejaculates; then, often, lovemaking is over. Tantric lovers build to a peak, then stop, level off, and circulate their energy, then build to another peak, and so on. Next week you'll learn about circulating energy, but today you'll get a taste of those peaks. Twice while making love, when excitement is high, stop and breathe for three minutes:

- The first time, lie still together and breathe in harmony, inhaling and exhaling together. The man sets the rhythm. Squeeze your PC muscles as you breathe.

- The second time, the woman sets the rhythm. Breathe in a circular rhythm, inhaling and exhaling opposite each other. Squeeze your PC muscles as you breathe.

Arrange a signal beforehand for beginning these breathing practices. It can be verbal, touch, or whatever is clearest for you both. For instance, a simple "Let's breathe together now" or three taps on the right shoulder.

Thought for the Day

Read this aloud:

Your intention is to merge with your lover in all aspects: body, mind, heart, and soul—not just body. As you open to the possibility of connection on all levels and let go of the goal of physical orgasms, you actually begin to have more of them.

Ending Your Practice

Finish your sacred loving time with a verbal thank-you to each other, followed by a head-to-toe hug for two minutes. Talk about your experience, particularly what it was like for you to incorporate conscious breath into your sexual activity. If you don't have time now, have a conversation about it later.

WEEK 3

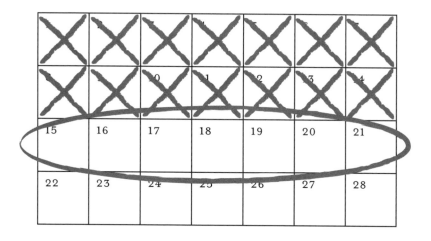

Congratulations! You've reached the midway point of your practice. This week you'll be learning about building a high energy charge and how to move it through your body. You'll add visualization, sound, and movement to your conscious breath and PC squeezes.

- Read through the full day's practice before you begin.

- Choose which partner will be today's guide.

- Time required for reading the exercises and practicing them: twenty minutes

Body Scan and Grounding

Time: four minutes

1. Body scan for one minute.

2. Ground for three minutes.

Looks of Love

Time: two minutes

From this point on, you'll decide between you who goes first with your daily loving gaze rather than have us tell you. Decide which partner will go first in the looks of love *before* you begin any of the daily practices.

Harmonized Breath, Visualization, and PC Pumping

Time: six minutes

Today you'll be adding visualization to your breathing practice. You'll picture energy flowing through your body, carried on the wave of your breath.

1. Sit or lie comfortably facing each other. Close your eyes.

2. With the woman setting the rhythm, begin harmonized breathing, inhaling and exhaling at the same time. Do five breaths together.

3. On the sixth breath, as you inhale, focus on bringing love into your body. Your breath carries it down through the center of your

body—in through your nose, to your throat, to your heart, to your solar plexus, to your belly, and finally to your genitals. Picture it as a golden light. Feel it as a wave of warmth.

4. As you exhale, the bright, golden wave of love rises up from your genitals and passes through your belly, your solar plexus, your heart, and your throat. It flows out through your nose toward your partner and into the universe.

5. Continue inhaling and exhaling love.

6. On the eleventh breath, add PC squeezes. Your pumping action magnifies the intensity of sensation and helps spread the loving energy through your whole system. Do fifty-five squeezes, as you did last week. Your breathing matches your partner's. Your PC squeezes are done at your own rate.

7. If you lose track of any part of the process, gently bring yourself back with an encouraging mental hug.

The Power of Sound

Sound carries energy. It frees blockages and helps you let go of control. Making sound opens your throat energy center—the center of creativity. Sound vibrates your body, moving it more freely toward orgasmic pleasure.

Today you'll experiment with three brief exercises to help you begin the process of making conscious sound during lovemaking. Sit up for these exercises. You can be side by side or facing each other—whatever will be easiest for you to focus.

HUMMING

Time: one minute

1. Inhale slowly and deeply through your nose.

2. Exhale slowly through your nose. Keep your mouth closed.

3. As you exhale, make a humming sound in your throat.

4. Repeat four more times. Feel the vibration.

AHHH

Time: one minute

1. Inhale slowly and deeply through your nose.

2. Exhale slowly through your mouth.

3. As you exhale, make a slow "Ahhh." Let it come up from deep in your belly. Feel it in your body as you let it go. This is the ancient sound of the great mother.

4. Repeat four more times.

OM

Time: two minutes

"OM" is the essential sound of the creative force of the cosmos. As you chant "OM," your energy harmonizes with the universal energy. To chant "OM," you divide it into three sounds that roll together: "Ahhh, Ohhh, Mmmm."

1. Inhale slowly and deeply.

2. Exhale through your mouth in three smooth stages, as follows:

    a. Make the sound "Ahhh," feeling it come from deep in your belly.

    b. Move to "Ohhh," feeling it flow up from your heart.

    c. Finish with "Mmmm," vibrating it in your throat.

3. Repeat nine more times.

Thought for the Day

Read this aloud:

Some people naturally make sound during lovemaking. For others it's very difficult at first, but with practice you'll become more free. As you get more and more excited, make lots of sounds. You can moan, groan, yell, scream, chant, sing, growl, and make animal noises. The louder and stronger the sound you make, the more that sound will carry your sexual energy with it, up and away from your genitals.

Ending Your Practice

End your fifteenth day of Tantra practice together with a full head-to-toe hug and a thank-you to each other and yourself.

- Read through the full day's practice before you begin.

- Choose which partner will be today's guide.

- Time required for reading the exercises and practicing them: twenty minutes

- Additional properties needed: music with a slow, steady, rhythmic beat for pelvic rocking (optional)

Body Scan and Grounding

Time: four minutes

1. Body scan for one minute.

2. Ground for three minutes.

Looks of Love

Time: two minutes

Harmonized Breath, Visualization, and PC Pumping

Time: six minutes

Repeat as yesterday with two differences:

- Today the man sets the breathing rhythm.

- Add humming sounds as you exhale (see yesterday's "Humming" practice).

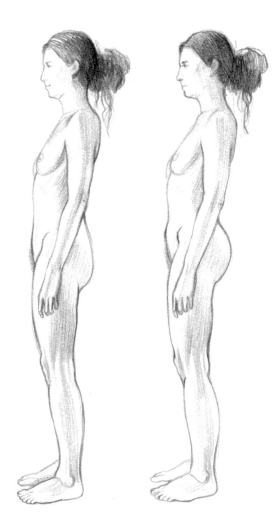

Pelvic Rocking

Time: three minutes

A loose pelvis plays a big part in moving energy through your system and intensifying your orgasmic response. Muscles that join your tailbone to your hips can become tight through lack of use. Pelvic rocking frees them up again. While the motion may appear subtle, as it does here, it should feel pronounced: let your pelvis tilt back distinctly, then snap it forward. (Or it may not be so subtle: watch John Travolta in *Grease* for the ultimate example.)

If you're using music for this exercise, start it now.

1. Stand beside each other about eighteen inches apart, facing in the same direction.

2. Set your feet shoulder-width apart, bend your knees slightly, and place your hands on your hips. Your eyes can be closed or open, whichever works best for you.

3. Rock your pelvis backward and forward, letting it swing freely: it's a vertical version of the thrusting motions of intercourse. Your upper body remains relaxed and still, and your feet stay flat on the floor, as your pelvis tips smartly back and snaps crisply forward.

4. After thirty seconds, add breathing to your rocking. Exhale as you rock your pelvis forward. Inhale as you rock back. Inhale through your nose. Exhale through your mouth.

5. After thirty seconds, add PC squeezes to your rocking and breathing. Contract your PC muscles as you tilt your pelvis forward and exhale. Relax your PC muscles as you swing your pelvis back and inhale.

6. After thirty seconds, add sound to your exhale. Make a strong "Ahhh" sound through your mouth. Let it come from deep inside you, from your genitals and belly. Feel the sound magnified and carried up through your body with every squeeze.

7. When you stop rocking, stand still for a moment, slow your breathing, and do a quick body scan. What do you notice?

If you become lightheaded during your rocking and breathing, slow your pace.

Thought for the Day

Read this aloud:

At first, the disciplined learning of sacred sex practices might feel awkward, uncomfortable, or scary. There's almost always a period of such frustration, in which learners want to conclude, "This doesn't work. I can't do it. This is too hard." They want to quit. But with persistence and some faith, a breakthrough arrives. They finally "get it." When you "get it," what seemed ridiculously complex and impossibly difficult becomes easy, like riding a bike. Once you can do it, you can always do it. You never forget.

Ending Your Practice

End your sixteenth day of Tantra practice together with a full head-to-toe hug and a thank-you to each other and yourself.

- Read through the full day's practice before you begin.

- Choose which partner will be today's guide.

- Time required for reading the exercises and practicing them: twenty minutes

- Additional properties needed: music with a slow, steady, rhythmic beat for pelvic rocking (optional)

Body Scan and Grounding

Time: four minutes

1. Body scan for one minute.

2. Ground for three minutes.

Looks of Love

Time: two minutes

Circular Breath, Visualization, and PC Pumping

Time: six minutes

1. Sit or lie facing each other. Your eyes can be open or closed, whichever way you can best focus together.

2. With the woman setting the rhythm, begin circular breathing. As she inhales, he exhales. Complete five breaths this way.

3. Beginning with the sixth breath, as you inhale, focus on bringing love into your body, through your nose down to your genitals, in a golden wave of light that rides on your breath.

4. As you exhale, this golden wave of love rises up from your genitals, passing out through your nose toward your partner.

5. Continue inhaling and exhaling love. Make humming sounds as you exhale.

6. On the eleventh breath, add PC pumps. Continue to breathe with your partner in the circular pattern, but do your fifty-five squeezes in whatever combination you individually want.

Pelvic Rocking

Time: three minutes
Repeat yesterday's practice.

Thought for the Day

Read this aloud:

Tantra is about opening and transformation. Like most spiritual paths, sacred sex teaches a discipline of the mind and body. It does so amid joy and letting go into the sensual aspects of living.

Ending Your Practice

End your seventeenth day of Tantra practice together with a full head-to-toe hug and a thank-you to each other and yourself.

- Read through the full day's practice before you begin.

- Choose which partner will be today's guide.

- Time required for reading the exercises and practicing them: twenty minutes

- Additional properties needed: music with a slow, steady, rhythmic beat for pelvic rocking (optional)

Body Scan and Grounding

Time: four minutes

1. Body scan for one minute.

2. Ground for three minutes.

Looks of Love

Time: two minutes

Circular Breath, Visualization, and PC Pumping

Time: five minutes

Repeat yesterday's practice with the following variations:

- Do forty-five PC squeezes today—three sets of fifteen.

- The man sets the rhythm.

Pelvic Rocking with Sound and Visualization

Time: five minutes

1. Stand beside each other. Set your feet shoulder-width apart, bend your knees slightly, and place your hands on your hips. Your eyes can be open or closed, whichever feels best for you.

2. Rock your pelvis back and forth. Exhale through your mouth as you tilt your pelvis forward. Inhale through your nose as you swing your pelvis back.

3. After thirty seconds, add PC pumps to your rocking and breathing. Contract as you tilt forward, and relax as you swing back.

4. After thirty seconds, add sound: "Ahhh." Let it come from deep inside you as you exhale.

5. After thirty seconds, add visualization with your rocking, breathing, squeezing, and sound.

   - As you rock forward and squeeze, visualize sending a ball of golden light from your genitals up the middle of your body to the center of your belly, an inch or two below your navel. Place your hands on your belly to help you focus. Do five pelvic rocks and breaths, sending golden light to your belly from your genitals.

   - For the next five rocks, breaths, squeezes, and sounds, send the golden ball from your genitals through your belly to your solar plexus—the center of your body, just below your rib cage. Place your hands on your solar plexus to help you focus.

   - For the next five rocks, breaths, squeezes, and sounds, send the golden ball from your genitals through your belly and your solar plexus to your heart center— the middle of your body, between your breasts (between the nipples for men). Place your hands on your heart center to help you focus.

   - For the next five rocks, send the golden ball from your genitals through your belly, your solar plexus, and your heart to your throat center—the middle of your throat. Place your hands on your throat center to help you focus.

   - For the next five, send the golden ball from your genitals through your belly, your solar plexus, your heart, and your throat to your third eye center—the middle of your forehead, just above your eyebrows. Place your hands here to help you focus.

- For the next five, send the golden ball from your genitals through your belly, your solar plexus, your heart, your throat, and your third eye to your crown energy center—on the top of your head, in the middle. Place your hands here to help you focus.

- For the next five, send the golden ball from your genitals through your belly, your solar plexus, your heart, your throat, your third eye, and your crown into the cosmos above you. Hold your hands above your head to help you focus.

6. Stop moving. Slow your breath.

7. Stay still for one minute as you scan your body. Then ground the energy, sending it down through your body into the earth. Allow calm, strength, and sensual vitality to flow up into you.

Thought for the Day

Read this aloud:

Maintain lifelong sexual fitness with a daily practice of pelvic rocking and PC pumping. You will gain muscle strength, improved circulation, and heightened sensitivity.

Ending Your Practice

End your eighteenth day of Tantra practice together with a full head-to-toe hug and a thank-you to each other and yourself.

- Read through the full day's practice before you begin.
- Choose which partner will be today's guide.
- Time required for reading the exercises and practicing them: twenty minutes
- Additional properties needed: music with a slow, steady, rhythmic beat for pelvic rocking (optional)

Body Scan and Grounding

Time: four minutes

1. Body scan for one minute.
2. Ground for three minutes.

Looks of Love

Time: two minutes

Circular Breath, Visualization, and PC Pumping

Time: five minutes
Repeat exactly as yesterday, but today the woman sets the rhythm.

Pelvic Rocking with Your Partner— Standing

Time: five minutes

- Repeat the steps of yesterday's pelvic-rocking practice, but today stand facing your partner about eighteen inches apart.
- Look at each other with soft eyes as you rock together.
- The woman sets the rhythm. The man matches her rocking, breathing, squeezing, sounds, and hand movements. Both of you inhale and exhale at the same time.
- When you've finished rocking, stand still, slow your breath, close your eyes, and do a body scan and grounding for one minute.

Thought for the Day

Read this aloud:

Sacred sex goes far beyond the bedroom, helping partners open fully to each other in trust and love through all facets of their relationship. Your relationship itself becomes a vehicle for spiritual growth and personal awareness. As you learn to open to yourself, to your own inner lover, you naturally open to others around you. You begin to understand that surrender does not mean submission or loss of self, but rather a loving expansion to something that is much greater than you are.

Ending Your Practice

End your nineteenth day of Tantra practice together with a full head-to-toe hug and a thank-you to each other and yourself.

- Read through the full day's practice before you begin.

- Choose which partner will be today's guide.

- Time required for reading the exercises and practicing them: twenty minutes

- Additional properties needed (optional): music with a slow, steady, rhythmic beat for pelvic rocking

Body Scan and Grounding

Time: four minutes

1. Body scan for one minute.

2. Ground for three minutes.

Looks of Love

Time: two minutes

Circular Breath, Visualization, and PC Pumping

Time: five minutes
Repeat exactly as yesterday, but today the man sets the rhythm.

Pelvic Rocking with Your Partner

Time: five minutes
Repeat the steps of yesterday's pelvic-rocking practice, but today the man sets the rhythm.

Thought for the Day

Read this aloud:

Few things could be as important to your happiness as a relationship that satisfies through and through, and healthy, passionate sexuality is one of the most important keys to relationship success. Equally important, commitment in a long-term relationship seems to be essential to create a moral legitimacy for passionate sex. The simple, but not necessarily easy, recipe is: relationship commitment + passionate sex = enduring happiness. But remember, great sex is much more than bodies rubbing delightfully together. It's also about trust, intimacy, and communication.

Ending Your Practice

End your twentieth day of Tantra practice together with a full head-to-toe hug and a thank-you to each other and yourself.

TANTRA LOVING SESSION THREE

Moving Energy

- Read through the entire practice before you begin.

- Time required for reading the exercises and practicing them: three hours

- Additional properties needed:

  - items for creating your sacred space (see list on Day 7)
  - five candles and matches or lighter
  - massage oils or lotions
  - music for pelvic rocking (optional)
  - firm pillows to sit on

Today you'll experiment with building a high sexual charge through manual and oral stimulation. When you reach a peak of sexual arousal, rather than releasing that energy in a regular orgasm, you'll play with moving it through your body. When your charge builds high enough, your whole body can become orgasmic. Depending on your sensitivity to energy, that may happen today or it may not happen for some time to come. Don't judge yourself; hug yourself. Let yourself laugh about it. Don't aim for a specific outcome; enjoy the journey. Focus completely on being in the moment, opening your heart to your lover, and fully experiencing whatever sensations come your way.

Body Scan and Grounding

Time: four minutes

1. Body scan for one minute.

2. Ground for three minutes.

Commitment Check

Time: two minutes

Talk to each other about the commitment you made at the beginning of this program. Has it become easier for you to maintain your practice as you continue, or more difficult? Look at how far you've come together in such a short time. You're magnificent!

Looks of Love and Invitation

Time: three minutes

After your two minutes of loving looks, the woman invites the man to embark on this loving adventure with her.

Creating Your Sacred Space

Time: twenty-five minutes

Create your sacred sensual space for lovemaking. Refer to Day 14's instructions if you need a refresher.

- As part of today's activities, you'll be giving each other a massage, so be sure to include a massage area in your setup.

- Incorporate an invitation to take part in this wonderful journey of Tantric awakening as part of the ritual of creating your space.

- You can include the walking in a circle ceremony from last week, or leave it out and proceed directly to today's ritual.

The Four Directions Ceremony

Four directions ceremonies are part of many celebratory traditions. Here's a version you can use to purify your lovers' room and to bring the qualities associated with the directions into your sexual play.

1. Place one candle at the perimeter of the room in each of the four directions: north, south, east, and west.

2. Move to the middle of the room. One of you holds the fifth candle as the other lights it. This candle represents the Source—the light of life, the universal energy. You'll light the other four candles from this one, in turn. As you light this candle, slowly and thoughtfully say together, "With this light, we connect to the Source, to the power of the All, to our Higher Selves and the Divine."

3. Move to the candle in the east. East represents the element air and the power of the mind—ideas, inspiration, and communication. Face east as you light this candle and say together, "With this light, we bring inspiration to our lovers' time. We communicate clearly and honestly. We use the power of our minds to focus our thoughts in this magical moment—here and now, together."

4. Move to the south candle, which represents the element fire and the power of action—desire, passion, power, and will. As you face south and light the candle, say together, "This light fires our passion. We act to create union through pleasure. We merge in the joyful heat of desire."

5. Move to the west candle—the element water and the power of emotion and transformation. As you face west and light the candle, say together, "With this light, we dive deep into the waters of our emotions. We dare to be vulnerable, transparent, and real. We open our hearts freely and fully to each other."

6. Move to the north candle—the element earth and the power of the body, the physical reality of your senses. As you face north and light the candle, say together, "With this light, we awaken all our senses. We allow our bodies to give and receive limitless pleasure. We offer our bodies to each other as divine gifts of ecstasy."

7. Finish this ceremony with a heartfelt embrace.

Sacred Bathing

Time: twenty-five minutes

Playfully and respectfully, share a bath or shower together. Refer to Day 14 to refresh your memory.

Reciprocal Massage

Time: forty-five minutes

Massage is a sensual, loving activity that relaxes your mind and body and helps you to be in the present and be connected to each other. Energy flows more freely through your system when you are at ease physically and mentally.

1. She gives him a massage first. You can refer to the instructions for a foot massage given on Day 9 and the instructions for a back rub given on Day 11 if you feel a little unsure about how to touch. Pace yourself so that you cover his full body in about twenty minutes. Warm the massage lotion in your hands before you apply it to his body. A very important point for the masseur to remember: focus on sending your love through your hands as you rub, knead, and stroke him. Be present!

2. Start with him on his belly and work from his feet up to his head. Make long, firm stroking motions up his body, using your fingers, thumbs, palms, and full hand. Men generally like a fair bit of pressure, particularly on the large muscle groups in the upper thighs, buttocks, back, and shoulders. Ask for feedback about pressure, speed, and areas of attention.

3. Ask him to roll over onto his back, and work your way up his body from his feet to his head. Massaging from the bottom up will relax his muscles but will also invigorate him for your sexy activities to come.

4. Switch roles. He gives and she receives. Women often like less pressure than men, so make sure you communicate clearly.

Pelvic Rocking with Your Partner—Sitting

Time: four minutes

Start building your charge with pelvic rocking. Today you'll be sitting.

- Sit facing each other on firm pillows with your legs crossed comfortably. Your knees can be touching if you want.

- With the woman setting the rhythm, repeat the steps you've previously learned: rocking, harmonized breathing, squeezing, making sounds, eye gazing, positioning your hands, and sending golden energy up through your body.

- When you've completed your rocking, do not ground the energy. Carry it with you into your next practice.

Building and Moving Your Hot Sexual Energy

Time: sixty minutes

You'll take turns pleasuring each other, manually and then orally, to build and move your sexual charge. He pleasures her first, manually.

1. Be sure to begin with kisses and caresses at her extremities—feet, hands, shoulders, neck, ears, mouth—then work your way inward to her hot spots. Women have erogenous zones all over their bodies that generally need to be awakened before their yonis come alive for pleasurable touch.

2. When you reach her genitals, also work from the outside in. With very light touches, teasingly awaken her groin creases, her anus, her perineum, her outer lips, and her inner lips before you stimulate her clitoris or put a finger inside her. She may want you to use some lubricant: saliva, water-based lubricant, or her own vaginal juices are best.

3. If you're not sure exactly how she likes her clitoris stroked, ask her to show or tell you. When you find a stroke that is particularly pleasing, keep doing it *exactly* the same way. Do not change anything—the

speed, the pressure, the location—unless she asks you to.

4. Help her build to a high peak of sexual arousal. Before she goes over into orgasm, do the following:

   • Stop your stimulation but keep your hands gently on her yoni, sending love to her in your touch. It may work best if she tells you when to stop. "Now" is a simple signal.

   • Ask her to make eye contact and to match you in a slow, harmonized breathing rhythm.

   • For one minute, she keeps her body relaxed as she squeezes her PC muscles, sending the hot charge up through her body.

   • She visualizes a golden light pulsing up through her with each squeeze.

   • To help move the energy, she also runs her hands lightly up her body from her yoni up past the top of her head.

5. Rest in stillness for a moment, breathing in harmony together. Feel your connection. Feel the divine energy flow.

Next, she pleasures him manually.

1. The head, or glans, of his penis is much more sensitive than the shaft, which has fewer nerve endings. As you caress him manually, vary the location, speed, and pressure of your strokes to build his excitement at a manageable pace.

2. Try a combination of six short, firm strokes along the shaft with six long, looser strokes that begin at the base of the lingam and slide along its full length, past and off the head. Make a slight twisting motion, the "corkscrew," as you glide past the head.

3. Be sure to pay some loving attention to his testicles, perineum, and anus.

4. Help him build to a high peak of sexual arousal. Before he goes over into orgasm, do the following:

   • Stop your stimulation but keep your hands gently on his genitals, sending love in your touch. It may work best if he indicates when to stop. "Now" is a simple signal.

   • Ask him to make eye contact and to match you in a slow, harmonized breathing rhythm.

- For one minute, he keeps his body relaxed as he squeezes his PC muscles, sending the hot charge up through his body.
- He visualizes a golden light pulsing up through him with each squeeze.
- To help move the energy, he also runs his hands lightly up his body from his lingam up past the top of his head.
- Rest in stillness for a moment, breathing in harmony. Feel your connection. Feel the divine energy flow.

Repeat the sequence with oral pleasuring, first for her and then for him.

If you wish to have an orgasm after practicing your energy movement, by all means go ahead, by whatever method you wish. But it will help your learning if you experiment with carrying this sexual charge instead of releasing it right away in a genitally focused orgasm. If you weren't intending to have an orgasm, but one comes upon you, let yourself go into it. Do not judge yourself. You are learning sexual mastery, and that takes time. Celebrate each orgasm. Laugh. Hug each other. Enjoyment makes learning easier.

Perineum Massage for Him

Time: two minutes

Give him a perineum massage to disperse any excess energy that may have accumulated in his genitals. This is especially important if he's chosen not to end this lovemaking session with an ejaculation.

Thought for the Day

Read this aloud:

Although Tantric loving lasts several hours, this does not mean you're having active intercourse during that entire time. Intercourse is interspersed with touching, oral play, and quietly holding each other. It's a good idea for a man to allow his erection to subside every thirty minutes, in order to exchange the blood supply and recharge his hormone levels.

Ending Your Practice

Finish your sacred loving time with a verbal thank-you to each other, followed by a head-to-toe hug for two minutes. Talk about your experience, particularly what it was like to postpone orgasm and endeavor to move your sexual energy. If you don't have time now, have a conversation about it later.

WEEK 4

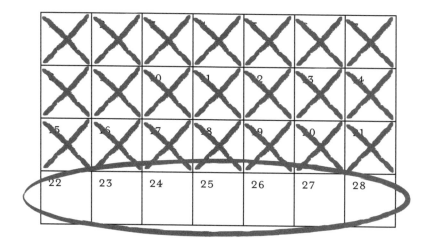

This week you'll continue building your energy and begin learning to circulate it with your partner. Woo-hoo!

- Read through the full day's practice before you begin.

- Choose which partner will be today's guide.

- Time required for reading the exercises and practicing them: twenty minutes

- Additional properties needed:
  - firm pillows to sit on
  - music (optional)

Body Scan and Grounding

Time: four minutes

1. Body scan for one minute.

2. Ground for three minutes.

Looks of Love

Time: two minutes

Love Talk

Time: five minutes

You've been sending your partner love with your eyes. Now you'll say it with words. As you're talking, you'll also be squeezing your PC muscles, in whatever manner you wish. This helps you make PC squeezing an automatic activity that you can do while your main focus is elsewhere—a talent you'll require to help you move your energy during lovemaking.

1. With your eyes closed, take one minute to reflect on how much your mate means to you. Consider your partner's finest quali-

ties—the attributes that you respect and admire and the elements that fire your desire.

2. Open your eyes and hold hands.

3. The man speaks first. For two minutes, he tells his lover all that is in his heart. He squeezes his PC muscles as he talks, but he keeps his focus on his feelings for her.

4. The woman speaks and squeezes second.

Pelvic Rocking with Your Partner— Sitting

Time: five minutes
Repeat yesterday's exercise, with the following variations:

- The man sets the rhythm.
- Do a one-minute body scan and grounding after your pelvic rocking.

Thought for the Day

Read this aloud:

When you look at your mate, look for the best. Seek the highest, greatest, most glorious aspects, especially when you are about to make love. Look for the god and goddess behind his or her eyes. You can never tell your mate too many times how much you admire him or how much you adore her. Hearing about the wonderful qualities your partner sees in you inspires you to bring those aspects of yourself out more often.

Ending Your Practice

End your twenty-second day of Tantra practice together with a full head-to-toe hug and a thank-you to each other and yourself.

- Read through the full day's practice before you begin.

- Choose which partner will be today's guide.

- Time required for reading the exercises and practicing them: twenty minutes

- Additional properties needed:
  - firm pillows to sit on
  - music (optional)

Body Scan and Grounding

Time: four minutes

1. Body scan for one minute.

2. Ground for three minutes.

Looks of Love

Time: two minutes

Pelvic Rocking with Your Partner— Sitting

Time: four minutes

Repeat yesterday's exercise, with the following variations:

- The woman sets the rhythm.

- When you've finished your rocking, do not do a body scan. Rather, move directly into the next practice.

Energy Circle in the Yab Yum

Time: five minutes

Today you'll be experimenting with circling energy between you in the Yab Yum, which is *the* Tantric love position. You're working up to sharing energy during intercourse in your lovers' time on Day 28.

In the Yab Yum position, the woman sits on the man's lap. It's important that you both be comfortable sitting together so that you can focus on circulating energy and not be distracted by discomfort in your back or thighs.

Experiment with the following sitting positions and determine which one you're most comfortable with *before* you begin any of today's exercises. The following are options for you to try:

- If he's a flexible yoga practitioner, he can sit cross-legged or in the lotus position.

- He can sit cross-legged with very firm pillows under his knees for support.

- He can sit on the bed or floor with his legs stretched straight out in front of him and with support behind his back.

- He can sit on an armless, straight-backed chair.

- She can sit on his lap with her legs wrapped around him.

- She can kneel over him, supporting some of her weight with her thighs.

1. After your pelvic rocking, move into your chosen sitting position.

2. When you're seated comfortably, close your eyes and begin circular breathing.

3. The woman sets the rhythm: she inhales, he exhales, she exhales, he inhales.

4. On the sixth breath, begin visualizing sharing energy between you in this way:

   a. As the man slowly exhales, he focuses on sending energy from his genitals into her genitals. Picture energy flowing in a golden stream.

   b. As the woman inhales, she draws that energy in through her genitals and up through the center of her body to her heart chakra, between her breasts.

   c. As she exhales, she sends the golden energy stream through her heart center into his heart center.

   d. As he inhales, he draws the energy in through his heart and down to his genitals.

   e. It may help you feel your heart chakra if you place your hand in the center of your partner's chest.

5. Continue the flow of this energy circle for three minutes.

6. When you've finished, sit in stillness for one minute and do a body scan.

Thought for the Day

Read this aloud:

Newness, freshness, and surprise are to be found in exploring the depths of your own and your lover's spiritual beings. Sex is one way to do this. You do not need to find a new lover; you only need to find new knowledge and skill about loving—a pursuit most suited to a lover you feel comfortable and safe with.

Ending Your Practice

End your twenty-third day of Tantra practice together with a full head-to-toe hug and a thank-you to each other and yourself.

- Read through the full day's practice before you begin.

- Choose which partner will be today's guide.

- Time required for reading the exercises and practicing them: twenty minutes

- Additional properties needed:
  - firm pillows to sit on
  - music (optional)

Body Scan and Grounding

Time: four minutes

1. Body scan for one minute.

2. Ground for three minutes.

Looks of Love

Time: two minutes

Pelvic Rocking with Your Partner— Sitting

Time: four minutes
Repeat yesterday's exercise, with the man setting the rhythm.

Energy Circle in the Yab Yum

Time: five minutes
Repeat this exercise exactly as you did it yesterday.

Thought for the Day

Read this aloud:

People who regularly experience pleasure are healthier and happier than others. Sex is one of the most natural ways to experience pleasure. A committed long-term relationship legitimizes sex and offers the needed safety and security to help you open to the many delights of sexual pleasure. Pleasure then becomes a universal, uplifting, and healing experience that brings you closer to each other and to God, rather than an individual craving that sets you apart and drives you deeper into selfishness.

Ending Your Practice

End your twenty-fourth day of Tantra practice together with a full head-to-toe hug and a thank-you to each other and yourself.

- Read through the full day's practice before you begin.

- Choose which partner will be today's guide.

- Time required for reading the exercises and practicing them: twenty minutes

Body Scan and Grounding

Time: four minutes

1. Body scan for one minute.

2. Ground for three minutes.

Harmonized Breath and PC Pumping

Time: three minutes

1. Sit or lie facing your partner.

2. Breathe in harmony together as you squeeze your PC muscles forty times in whatever combination you individually choose. The man sets the breathing rhythm.

Looks of Love

Time: two minutes

Pelvic Rocking with Your Partner in the Yab Yum Position

Time: three minutes

1. Sit in whichever variation of the Yab Yum position is most comfortable for you.

   Note: If you find you can't do the pelvic rocking comfortably together with the woman in the man's lap, try this variation:

   - Sit facing each other on the floor (on firm pillows if you like), as close together as you can.

   - Keep your feet flat on the floor and knees bent. Make sure your legs are outside each other's hips.

   - Rock as described.

2. Your eyes can be open or closed, whichever works best to help you focus.

3. Begin to rock your pelvises back and forth together. Both of you rock toward each other at the same time and away from each other at the same time. The man sets the rhythm for all elements of the exercise.

4. Match your breathing, inhaling and exhaling at the same time.

5. Add "Ahhh" sounds to your exhale.

6. After five "Ahhhs," add PC squeezes to your rocking. Visualize energy moving up through your body with each squeeze.

7. Run your hands lightly up your partner's back to help the energy flow.

8. After three minutes, stop rocking; the man decides when to stop. Move directly into the next practice.

Energy Circle in the Yab Yum

Time: four minutes

1. Stay in the Yab Yum position.

2. Begin circular breathing with the man leading. He inhales, she exhales.

3. On the sixth breath, do as follows:
   - He exhales and sends energy through his genitals into hers.
   - She inhales and draws the energy up to her heart.
   - She exhales and sends the energy into his heart.
   - He inhales and draws the energy down to his genitals.

4. Continue for three minutes.

5. When you have finished, sit in stillness for one minute and do a body scan.

Thought for the Day

Read this aloud:

Learning to circulate hot sexual energy is not really difficult, but it takes discipline and practice. For instance, within a few days of trying some of the techniques in this plan, men will likely notice an improvement in their ability to delay ejaculation. Real mastery of sexual energy, however, takes months, even years, to achieve. But unlike childhood piano lessons, this is practice you'll look forward to.

Ending Your Practice

End your twenty-fifth day of Tantra practice together with a full head-to-toe hug and a thank-you to each other and yourself.

- Read through the full day's practice before you begin.
- Choose which partner will be today's guide.
- Time required for reading the exercises and practicing them: twenty minutes

Body Scan and Grounding

Time: four minutes

1. Body scan for one minute.
2. Ground for three minutes.

Harmonized Breath and PC Pumping

Time: three minutes
Repeat exactly as yesterday, but with the woman leading.

Looks of Love

Time: two minutes

Pelvic Rocking with Your Partner in the Yab Yum Position

Time: three minutes
Repeat as yesterday, but with the woman leading.

Energy Circle in the Yab Yum

Time: four minutes
Repeat as yesterday, but with the woman leading.

Thought for the Day

Read this aloud:

Lose weight. Reduce stress. Lower your cholesterol level. Improve your circulation. Live longer. Stay younger.

Sounds like an ad for a new wonder drug, right? In fact, it's a partial list of the benefits of humanity's oldest and most pleasurable pastime: sex. Healthy blood, healthy bones, healthy heart, healthy body, and a peaceful mind—all thanks to the healing powers of sex. Next time you're in the mood, let your lover know you've got the doctor on your side.

Ending Your Practice

End your twenty-sixth day of Tantra practice together with a full head-to-toe hug and a thank-you to each other and yourself.

- Read through the full day's practice before you begin.
- Choose which partner will be today's guide.
- Time required for reading the exercises and practicing them: twenty minutes

Body Scan and Grounding

Time: four minutes

1. Body scan for one minute.
2. Ground for three minutes.

Harmonized Breath and PC Pumping

Time: three minutes
Repeat as yesterday, but with the man leading.

Looks of Love

Time: two minutes

Pelvic Rocking with Your Partner in the Yab Yum Position

Time: three minutes
Repeat as yesterday, but with the man leading.

Energy Circle in the Yab Yum

Time: four minutes

- Repeat as yesterday, with the woman leading.
- When you have finished breathing together and circulating your energy, spend the last minute chanting "OM" together.

Thought for the Day

Read this aloud:

When you do find a particular stroke or caress that is really driving her wild, keep doing it and keep doing it and keep doing it. Don't change anything about it. Don't go faster, slower, softer, harder, or switch directions. Keep doing exactly the same thing until she lets you know she wants a change either through words or body movement. This holds true whether you're pleasuring her clitorally or vaginally, with your fingers or your mouth. Keep going even if your hands or mouth get tired.

Ending Your Practice

End your twenty-seventh day of Tantra practice together with a full head-to-toe hug and a thank-you to each other and yourself.

TANTRA LOVING SESSION FOUR

Lovers' Ritual

- Read through the entire practice before you begin.

- Time required for reading the exercises and practicing them: four hours

- Additional properties needed:

  - items for creating your sacred space (see list on Day 7)
  - one of the following: sweet grass, cedar, sage, or incense for purifying (or you can use a spray bottle filled with water mixed with your favorite essential oil)
  - a long sash, scarf, or ribbon, approximately four to six feet long
  - a candle
  - sensual clothing: erotic, sexy, special clothes that say "This is me"
  - slow, romantic music
  - tasty food tidbits, preferably finger foods, to feed each other, and your favorite beverages

Hooray! You've reached the final day of your twenty-eight-day Tantric sex journey. Congratulations!

Your entire lovemaking time today is a celebration of love, connection, and transcendence. Today, you are god and goddess and you'll honor yourself and one another as such. Throughout these hours, keep reminding yourself to allow your glory out and to encourage the magnificence of your lover.

Body Scan and Grounding

Time: four minutes

1. Body scan for one minute.
2. Ground for three minutes.

Commitment Check

Time: five minutes
Talk to each other about the commitment you made at the beginning of this program. How did you fare over these four weeks with your commitment? What has this time of learning and practice been like for you? Acknowledge and congratulate each other for reaching this last stage of your wondrous journey. You are truly magnificent!

Looks of Love and Invitation

Time: three minutes
After your two minutes of loving looks, the man invites the woman to embark on this loving adventure with him.

Creating Your Sacred Space

Time: twenty-five minutes
Create your sacred sensual space for lovemaking. Refer to Day 14's instructions if you need a refresher. You can use the ceremonies from Days 14 and 21 to energize and purify your space if you want to. Or, you can try the one below.

THE CONNECTION

- Both partners stand in the center of the room.
- The man lights the candle and holds it in his right hand. As he lights it, both say, "The light of the Source guides us to love."
- In his left hand, he holds one end of the ribbon.

- The woman then lights the "smoky" substance and holds it in her left hand, or she holds the water sprayer. She holds the other end of the ribbon in her right hand.

- He stays in the center of the room. She moves as far out to the perimeter as the ribbon and room allow.

- She walks slowly around the room in a clockwise direction, spreading the smoke or spraying the water. They say, "The light guides us, our love connects us, the fire [or water] clears our way."

Sacred Bathing

Time: twenty-five minutes
Playfully and respectfully, share a bath or shower together. Refer to Day 14 to refresh your memory.

Yin/Yang Dancing

Time: twenty minutes

- Dress in your special "this is me" clothing.

- Play three or four slow, romantic songs for slow dancing. You don't have to be a good dancer. It's not about impressing anyone, it's about making a sensual connection with your lover. All you need to do is hold each other and sway your body to the music.

- As the first song begins, the man starts leading his partner in the dance, in whatever way he chooses.

- After approximately one minute, he relinquishes the lead to the woman. He can say, "Your turn." She then leads for one minute and returns the lead to him.

- Continue on in this way, switching the lead back and forth.

Honoring Your Lover with Food and Drink

Time: twenty-five minutes

- Gather your prepared selection of food tidbits and beverages. Present them beautifully.

- Ask your lover if you may honor her or him with these bodily delights.

- Take turns feeding each other. Linger over each bite. Pass food from fingers to lips and from mouth to mouth.

- Allow yourself to savor the colors, the aromas, the textures, and the tastes of each morsel.

Sensual Disrobing

Time: twenty minutes

You can do either of the following:

- Do a slow, sexy striptease for your lover, one person at a time.

- Undress each other, one person at a time—very, very slowly and attentively.

Circular Breathing and PC Pumping

Time: five minutes

Tune in to each other and start your energy flowing with circular breathing and PC pumping.

- The woman sets the breathing rhythm.
- Do forty PC squeezes in whatever combination you like.

Awakening Your Goddess

Time: twenty minutes

The *Ananga Ranga*, a sixteenth-century Indian love manual, teaches that passion resides in different parts of a woman's body according to the cycle of the moon. You'll awaken your goddess passion with this ritual.

- Seat your goddess in front of you and kneel before her. Ask her permission to show your adoration and to awaken her passion.
- Start with the big toe on her right foot, lightly massaging it. Envision sending loving, arousing energy into her as you gently vibrate first your hands and then your lips on her toe.
- Apply the same loving touch and kiss to the rest of her body in this order: right foot, right knee, right thigh, yoni, right buttock, navel, middle of chest, right breast, right side, right side of throat, right cheek, lower lip, right eye, and top of her head.
- Then move to her left eye, upper lip, left cheek, left side of throat, left side, left

breast, middle of chest, navel, left buttock, yoni, left thigh, left knee, left foot, and left toe.

- She eagerly accepts your loving touch, and she encourages her body to awaken to it by focusing intently on each part as you touch it. She also rocks her pelvis gently and squeezes her PC muscles.

- When you have finished your journey over her body, move on to the next segment of your lovers' time.

Building to Orgasmic Peaks

Time: one hour

During this next hour, you will build to successive peaks of sexual arousal with combinations of manual and oral stimulation and intercourse. You can mix up the specific techniques you use, depending on your individual preferences. When you get to peaks of excitement, do the following:

FOR MANUAL AND ORAL STIMULATION

- Stop stimulation and still your bodies.

- Slow your breathing and breathe in circular rhythm.

- Make "Ahhh" or humming sounds on the breath exhale.

- Make eye contact, at least part of the time.

- Keeping your body relaxed, squeeze your PC muscles and send energy up through your body. Visualize it as a golden light if this helps you.

- Run your hands up your body, or your lover's body, to help move the energy.

FOR INTERCOURSE

- Move into the Yab Yum position, with genital penetration.

- Begin circular breathing.

- Send your hot sexual energy in the circle from genitals to heart and heart to genitals.

- Chant "OM" together as you circulate your energy.

- When your excitement begins to fade and/or the man's erection goes, you can rock, breathe, and squeeze rapidly together to rebuild your charge. Or, you can change to another intercourse position or sexual-arousal activity. Or, you can have a cuddly rest.

NOTES TO ASSIST YOU WITH THIS ENERGY-MOVING PRACTICE

- Endeavor to build to four or more peaks of arousal and energy movement.

- Decide beforehand what signal you'll use to change from building excitement to moving energy.

- Decide beforehand who will set the rhythm.

- Remember at all times that each of you is a divine spirit merging with another divine spirit. Remember it when you are in moments of quiet connection as well as when you are in a wild sexual frenzy.

- If the man ejaculates before you have reached the number of peaks you had planned to, be relaxed and easy with it. Let him rest for twenty minutes, and then see if he can arise again with attentive manual or oral stimulation. If not, you've got lots of time to practice another day.

Ending with the Lovers' Scissors

Time: ten minutes

Try to end this lovemaking session while you still have desire. (This is a suggestion, not a rule.) That means that your energy charge is high and that usually the man has not ejaculated. See what it is like to carry this extraordinary vibration with you. The Lovers' Scissors position is a fabulous one for ending your lovemaking. It's very comfortable for both of you, and you can maintain it much longer than ten minutes if you want to.

- The man lies on his left side, and the woman lies on her back.

- Your heads are apart, and your genitals are together. Your bodies are at a 90-degree angle to each other.

- The man's left leg is against the bed. The woman's left leg crosses on top of it. His

right leg crosses over her left. Then her right leg goes over his hip. This is the "scissors."

- You can make eye contact. You can rest a hand on your own or your lover's heart center.

- Breathe together in harmony.

- Focus on your genital connection. Feel the energy there and allow it to simply spread throughout your system.

Thought for the Day

Read this aloud:

Tantric lovemaking involves breathing exercises, muscle-contraction exercises, sound, visualization, affirmations, creating a sacred loving space and other rituals, meditation, sensual massage, and sexual play. In order to create enough sexual energy to move into ecstatic states of divine connection, Tantrikas make love for long periods of time, experiencing extraordinary levels of pleasure along the way.

Part of the delight of Tantric loving is that you can continue to learn and advance throughout years of practice; it is never-ending in its potential for growth. At the same time, it is a practice that yields immediate results. You will be able to see and feel a difference in your lovemaking experience right away if you follow these steps.

Ending Your Practice

Finish your sacred loving time with a verbal thank-you to each other. You can do this

- in the Lovers' Scissors, or

- in a head-to-toe hug.

Talk about your experience today and throughout the whole twenty-eight days. You've completed a powerful training in sacred sexuality, together. You're magnificent!

FOUR

Tantric Loving
Step by Step

This brief chapter outlines the eight elements of an extended sacred loving time. These elements are a guide to help you design your own very special times together. Insert activities from "The 28-Day Ecstasy Plan," as well as from chapter 5, "Ecstasy Recipe," and chapter 6, "Continuing Your Practice" (which lays out a plan for continuing your Tantric journey beyond the four weeks just detailed), into the various segments to create unique, uplifting, and ecstatic lovemaking sessions.

Intention

Regular lovemaking has a goal: orgasm. With sacred sex, there is no goal. There is a purpose, however, and that purpose is union. Your intention is to merge with your lover in all aspects: mind, heart, and soul as well as body. You can help this along by looking at your lover differently, by seeing your partner as a god or goddess, as a living expression of the Divine. Look for the glory, beauty, and wonder in your playmate and in yourself, and let that shine.

Creating a Sacred Space

For Tantric loving, you transform your regular space into sacred space. The important thing is your intention, not the specific items you use. Tidy the room. Change the lighting with candles or colored bulbs. Soften sharp edges by draping furniture with sumptuous fabrics. Bring in sensual objects, plants, tasty drinks and eats, and lots of pillows. After you've created the space, purify it energetically. Consciously send away negative or fearful thoughts and feelings and invite in those that are joyous, passionate, and safe. Speak these ideas aloud;

dare to step beyond your shyness or feelings of foolishness. Create your own purification rituals with sweet grass, incense, and musical instruments, or borrow from ancient traditions.

The Lovers' Purifying Bath

Cleanse each other in preparation for joyous union. Wash away the dirt and cares of the world in a hot bath with essential oils and bath salts, or a shared shower. Make it slow and luxurious, each of you giving complete attention to your lover. Wash and dry each other with playful abandon. Apply lotions and scents to prepare your bodies for the delights ahead.

Honor, Respect, and Permission

Trust, surrender, and opening your heart are essential if you want to reach the heights of bliss. It's not just technique that will get you there. You must join together as loving equals on the sexual journey. Tell your partner how magnificent he or she is, how much he or she attracts you, how much he or she inspires you, what it is about your lover that turns you on, and how good that is. Finally, ask permission to passionately love your partner in your practice of Tantric sex.

Tuning In to Sexual Play

After you've asked and received permission to love each other up, tune in to each other. Two simple ways to do this are by harmonizing your breathing and by looking deep into each other's eyes. By matching your breathing rhythms and making soulful eye contact, you connect energetically as well as physically. Use other connecting practices also, like massage, dance, reading poetry, or partner yoga.

Begin to explore each other's bodies with wonder, lust, and playfulness. Work from the outside in. Go very, very slowly. Take turns being the giver and the receiver. Use all your senses. Be daring and imaginative.

Going the Distance

Tantric lovemaking is extended over hours. Periods of lusty action are interspersed with quiet moments of loving stillness. Intercourse is mixed with touching, oral play, gently holding each other, massage, stimulating conversation, and feeding each other. Lovers build to high peaks of excitement, ride that wave, let the energy subside a bit, and then build again to higher and higher levels. Men delay ejaculation so they can build a high sexual charge and eventually learn to experience orgasm without ejaculation. Orgasm without ejaculation will not deplete the man's energy the same way that an ejaculatory orgasm does, so lovemaking can continue. It's a good idea for a man to allow his erection to subside every thirty to forty-five minutes to exchange the blood supply and recharge his hormone levels.

Moving and Sharing Your Energy

Riding the wave of bliss happens when lovers become totally aroused sexually and maintain that arousal for a period of time. They build up an enormous sexual and spiritual energy. With a combination of breathing, relaxation, and muscle-contraction exercises, both men and women learn to circulate sexual energy through their own and their lover's body. Ultimately, the ego boundaries disappear, and the lovers become one in ecstatic union.

At the peak of sexual arousal, either during intercourse or manual or oral stimulation, stop your normal lovemaking movements and focus on moving the sexual energy that's pulsing in your genitals. Move it up and through your body. Use slow, deep abdominal breathing to keep your body relaxed. Add the PC pumping action and visualize moving energy up your body in a ball of fire, a wave of light, or a current of electricity. Run your hands up your body and your lover's body to help the energy rise. Make sounds of love and meditation. Through your eyes, your hands, your genitals, and your voice, pass this powerful force on to your lover. At first, this may seem difficult, because we aren't accustomed to paying attention to our internal energy. With practice, you'll be able to recognize and direct it.

Afterplay

After you've gone to a number of successive peaks of arousal and energy movement (how many depends on your inclination and stamina as well as the time you have available), wind down your loving time with slow caresses, words of endearment, and honoring each other with food and drink. Stay connected, breathe in unison, look into each other's eyes, and revel in your deep connection. Thank each other for sharing this sacred time together.

FIVE

Ecstasy Recipe—
Your Joyous Steps to Bliss

ere are fifty new ways to please each other during your extended weekly loving times. They fit within the eight major elements of a Tantric playtime as outlined in chapter 4. Activities range from playful to profound and are presented in the following five categories:

- Relationship and Communication
- Sexual Technique and Skills
- Energy Work and Meditation
- Sexual Play and Fantasy
- Ritual and Ceremony

Relationship and Communication

1. GIVING AND RECEIVING

You may have been taught that it's nobler to give than to receive, but one of the greatest gifts you can give is to willingly, happily, receive your lover's attentions and offerings. Practice conscious giving and receiving with each other. Take turns, from time to time, to ask for what you want before you begin your extended loving session. Then, during your playtime, grant your lover's desires with pleasure. Receive your wishes graciously.

2. ANTICIPATION

Call your playmate several times during the day prior to your lovers' encounter. Talk of all the sexy, romantic, erotic things you have planned for your rendezvous.

3. TENDER TALK

Prepare ahead for intimate conversations you'll have when you're basking in the afterglow of climax. Make your topics personal and loving. This is not the time to talk about relationship issues, family problems, or other disagreements. Extend your state of sublime harmony with topics such as these:

- Tell your darling specific reasons why you love him or her.

- Speak of some of the things you admire about your lover.

- Remind each other of why being together is so important to you.

- Recall happy moments from early in your relationship.

- Share dreams for your future together.

- Tell each other what was splendid about the lovemaking you just created.

- Entertain your love with funny jokes and stories.

- Be completely transparent with the intensity of your feelings for your sweetheart. Name your feelings and describe them.

Sexual Technique and Skills

4. KAMA SUTRA SEX

Explore lovemaking the *Kama Sutra* way with the help of an illustrated guide, such as our *Complete Idiot's Guide to Supercharged Kama Sutra*. Select one or two of the more than thirty sexual intercourse positions to experiment with during your lovemaking. Do the same with techniques of kissing, hugging, scratching, biting, and slapping—all of which are presented in great detail in the *Kama Sutra*. Next, experiment with the hundreds of possible combinations of kissing, touching, and intercourse. Working your way through the entire *Kama Sutra* can give you months of stimulating sex-ploration.

5. POSITIONS FOR BUILDING EXCITEMENT

Positions that pair up opposite parts of the body—for example, top to bottom ("69," as on page 71) and front to back (rear-entry, as shown here)—build excitement and arousal quickly for both partners. These positions provide maximum stimulation to encourage a man's rock-hard erection. Be aware, though, that they can also lead to a quick ejaculation. They're great for short sessions of passionate loving and for men who have difficulty reaching an ejaculatory climax.

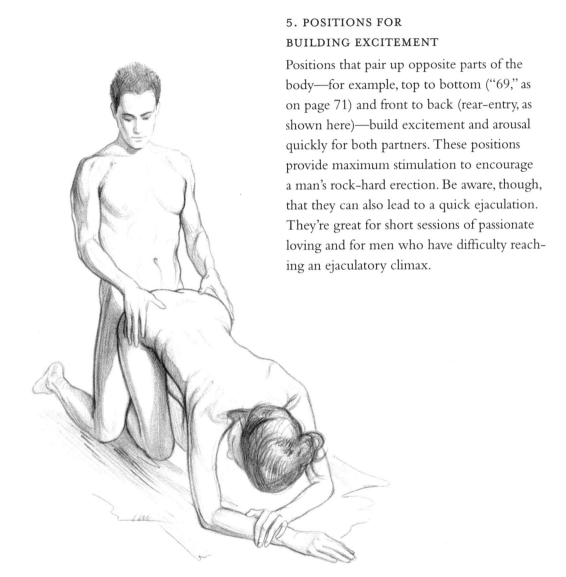

6. POSITIONS FOR EMOTIONAL CONNECTION

Face-to-face positions are the best for establishing an intense emotional connection. They're perfect for extended lovemaking and for those moments when you want to circulate, rather than continue to build, your hot sexual energy. Share your energy through your genital connection, eye contact, harmonized breathing, and kissing, in face-to-face positions.

7. BABY, YOU ARE TOPS!

During sexual intercourse, the lover on top gives the most energy to the lover on the bottom. If one of you is in a weakened condition—from an accident, illness, life stress, or work exhaustion—take the bottom spot. Also, the person on top is more dominant. Explore power issues in your relationship by taking turns surrendering on the bottom and assuming control on the top.

8-15. SLOW MOVE/DON'T MOVE

These eight sexual meditations are ideal for cultivating hot sexual energy, promoting sexual healing, and reuniting sex with spirit. They use full body relaxation, some PC squeezing, slow and deep breathing, harmonized breathing, and visualization to move sexual energy up from your genitals through the crown of your head, or to exchange it back and forth with your partner.

Although orgasm may come upon you, you're not trying to make it happen. In most of these meditations, there's no male ejaculation. These non-goal practices assist with healing from sexual abuse and help overcome sexual dysfunctions such as impotence, premature ejaculation, and inability to experience orgasm. They also unlock your door into the mysterious realm of spirit. These meditations do require effort, but the primary quality you bring is surrender, not control. You open to allow something to unfold rather than striving to make something happen.

As you begin your practice, delaying ejaculation may be difficult for you to do. This is common. Don't be hard on yourself; don't make ejaculation into a problem. Thoroughly enjoy and celebrate each ejaculation, whether you've intended it to happen or not. Over time your skill will grow, and eventually ejaculation will become completely voluntary. Then, these meditations will profoundly increase your sexual pleasure and add an astounding spiritual dimension to your lovemaking.

8.

Lie together, *without* penetration, for one hour. Look into each other's eyes, harmonize your breathing, and touch each other erotically—everywhere.

9.

With the lingam nestled inside the yoni, lie completely still together for one hour. Look into each other's eyes and breathe in rhythm together. No kissing, touching, or PC squeezing—just total stillness. If the penis slips out of the vagina, remain still and continue your emotional connection.

10.

For one hour, lie together with the lingam inside the yoni. Make loving eye contact and breathe together. Include PC squeezing—both partners or just the woman.

11.

With his lingam inside the yoni for one hour, the man thrusts just enough to maintain his erection. Look into each other's eyes, match your breathing, squeeze your PC muscles, and kiss and touch each other erotically.

12.

As soon as the lingam enters the yoni, begin rhythmic thrusting and continue for approximately ten minutes, or as long as you can without going over the edge. Become still, stay connected, and rest together for thirty minutes. Withdraw the penis for ten minutes. Repeat this sequence three or more times.

13.

Build to a peak of sexual arousal with foreplay and intercourse, but stop before the man ejaculates. Interrupt intercourse for other activities, explicitly sexual or not. Then build to another peak with intercourse, but once again stop before ejaculation. Over a period of several hours, build to at least four such peaks—aim for eight or ten—before ejaculation. Or, end lovemaking without ejaculating at all.

14.

Build to a peak of sexual arousal, but stop before the man ejaculates. Stay at that level of arousal, moving only enough to keep you at the edge of ejaculation. Some PC squeezing by one or both partners may be all the movement necessary to ride the wave of pleasure and turn the peak into a plateau. Stay at the plateau for twenty to sixty minutes. Interrupt the intercourse for other activities for at least ten minutes. Build to another peak and repeat one or more times.

15.
After the man ejaculates during a lovemaking session, remain genitally connected for twenty to thirty minutes so there can be a reabsorption of vital energies from the lovers' combined secretions.

16. TO EJACULATE OR NOT TO EJACULATE?
Men, find your personal answer to this question by observing how you feel after lovemaking when you (a) ejaculate, and (b) don't ejaculate, and end lovemaking while you still have desire. In both instances, compare how you feel

- immediately after lovemaking ends;
- one hour after lovemaking ends;
- several hours after lovemaking ends;
- the next day.

Keep a written record of differences using the following points as a guide:

1. Physical vitality: Are you sleepy, energized, exhausted, relaxed, depleted, lively?

2. Emotional vitality: Are you depressed, happy, angry, joyous, resentful, grateful, lonely, connected?

3. Libido: Do you feel
   - no desire for sex?
   - low desire for sex?
   - medium desire for sex?
   - high desire for sex?

   How long does it take before you start to desire sex again—minutes, hours, or days?

4. Erection: How much time passes before you can get another erection? On a scale of 1 to 10 (1 being easiest and 10 most difficult), how easy was it to get? On a scale of 1 to 10 (1 being partially erect and 10 rock hard), how firm is your erection?

5. Personal effectiveness: Is your performance at work, in sports, or in artistic pursuits enhanced or diminished? Consider factors like decision making, problem solving, creativity, endurance, and strength.

6. Affection: Do you feel like touching, hugging, kissing, and cuddling, or do you lose interest in affectionate behaviors?

7. Quality of ejaculatory orgasm: Does the frequency of ejaculation affect
   - the intensity of sensation during ejaculation?
   - how long an ejaculation lasts?
   - the quantity of your ejaculate?

8. Prostate gland: How does the frequency of ejaculation affect how your prostate feels? If you notice that your prostate becomes sore (feels heavy and/or aches) from delaying ejaculation, it usually means you haven't circulated sexual energy away from it. Allow yourself to ejaculate to restore your comfort; then you can safely resume your delaying practices.

9. Tension release: Do you use ejaculation to reduce tension? Do you feel relaxed after an ejaculation or "wiped out?" Are there other ways to relax and manage stress, or is ejaculation your preferred method?

10. Overall health status: Does frequency of ejaculation affect your general health? Check with the following six-month lovemaking experiment. For three months, ejaculate frequently—daily or every second day. For three months, ejaculate infrequently—once per week or once per month. To make your results comparable, make love approximately the same number of times during each three-month period.

17. ERECTION SIGNALS

Use your stage of erection to help you learn ejaculation mastery. Identify the four stages of erection.

- Stage 1: A limp penis; no erection, but you feel sensation in your penis and you're starting to think about sex.

- Stage 2: A partially erect but not fully erect penis.

- Stage 3: Fully erect but not completely engorged with blood.

- Stage 4: Fully engorged with blood. Stage 4 is harder, hotter, and a darker color than Stage 3.

Encourage your erection to come and go a number of times so you'll both be able to identify the stages. At peaks of sexual arousal, especially during active sexual intercourse, a

Stage 4 erection usually means that ejaculation is unpredictable and could happen in the blink of an eye. If you allow your erection to subside to Stage 3 or lower, you'll be able to last longer.

18. INTERNAL PROSTATE MASSAGE

A man's prostate is a key to the quality of his sexual experience. Massaging the prostate externally, through the perineum, is helpful, but internal prostate massage, through the anus, is best. Include an external prostate massage with every session of lovemaking and an internal prostate massage with lovemaking sessions that last an hour or more.

An internal prostate massage completely relaxes the prostate and allows any excess sexual energy to be released without an ejaculation. The prostate remains at ease, with no enlargement or hardness. When a man gains some mastery at moving his hot sexual energy, an at-ease prostate enables him to delay his ejaculation almost indefinitely, even with vigorous, active lovemaking, a Stage 4 erection, and full-force thrusting. Also, when a man allows himself to be penetrated anally, he must surrender completely. Surrender is a core competency in Tantric lovemaking.

Assume a position on all fours, with your head on your crossed arms and your buttocks in the air, or lie on your side, knees bent toward your chest. Wearing latex or vinyl gloves, your partner massages your anus with lots and lots of water or silicone-based lubricant. Using her longest finger, she teases her way inside very slowly and gently. She'll feel a lump, like a large grape or small walnut. She'll rub and circle it, firmly but gently, for two to three minutes and then slowly withdraw her finger. Wash up with soap and a warm, wet cloth.

19. MEN—MASTURBATION FOR EJACULATION MASTERY

Masturbation helps men learn about their sexual-arousal process and develop mastery over their ejaculation response. As a young male, you may have treated masturbation as a race to the finish line, completing the whole business after a minute or two of furious pumping. Now you'll take your time and look for body signals that warn you ejaculation is coming soon. Masturbate close to ejaculation—about 90 percent—and then back off, allowing your arousal and erection to subside. Resume building to another peak, then back off, and so on. Below are warning signals to watch for;

once you're aware of them, you'll always have a choice to continue on to ejaculation or to back off and delay it.

- You have a Stage 4 erection. However, most men can stay in Stage 4 longer during masturbation than they can during intercourse. This gives you a better opportunity to notice the other signals your body is presenting.

- Your upper torso, from your chest above the nipples to your face, flushes or darkens in color.

- Your breathing becomes rapid, rough, and irregular.

- You begin making uncontrollable sounds.

- Your testicles pull up into your body.

- You tense your entire body, contracting many muscle groups at the same time.

- You feel an internal sensation at the prostate, which signals the beginning of the orgasmic response.

20. WOMEN—MASTURBATION FOR BUILDING A HIGHER SEXUAL CHARGE

Women don't generally lose their sexual energy with an orgasm. In fact, when you're relaxed and orgasmic, one orgasm can lead to another and increase your desire for more sexual activity. But when you've learned to reach orgasm fairly easily through clitoral self-stimulation, it's time to start postponing orgasm and build a higher sexual charge. This will lead you to full-body orgasm and mystical, blissful states. Follow the steps below.

- Stimulate yourself lovingly to just before orgasm.

- Stop stimulation but maintain contact with your clitoris.

- Relax your body.

- Slow your breathing.

- Squeeze your PC muscles.

- Run one hand up your body, from your yoni to the crown of your head and above into the air.

- Visualize your sexual energy as a golden ball of heat that starts in your yoni and moves up through your body with your rhythmic PC squeezes and your hand motions.

- Repeat the process.

21. MAY I WATCH, PLEASE?

Inability to find the right words and shyness about asking for what you want can make it difficult to explain to your partner how you want to be touched. Masturbating while your lover watches shows your partner the touches you like, and it's also a great turn-on. So, put on a magnificent show. Set up the room as a sacred, sensuous space, just like you would for other extended loving sessions. Take your time. Men must choose whether their demonstration concludes with an ejaculation or acts as a prelude to partner sex.

22. VERY PERSONAL PLEASURE

There's a lot of negative conditioning attached to masturbation. Many associate it with feelings of shame and guilt. You may feel embarrassed that you're self-pleasuring instead of making love with a partner. But you're not

together all the time, and when you are, your partner may not always want to make love when you do. Self-pleasuring is a normal part of healthy sexuality. Make your masturbation sessions special by setting up the room as a sacred space with soft lighting and sensual music. Be sure you won't be disturbed—lock the door and turn off the phone. Allow yourself an hour or more to build to climax ever so slowly.

23. WOMEN—RELAXING INTO PLEASURE

At peaks of sexual excitement, rather than tightening up to hasten orgasm as many women have learned to do, experiment with relaxing your body. Staying relaxed doesn't mean being a limp noodle. It means that your body is not tight and tense, but that it is loose so that the energy can flow and the pleasure can course through you. Slow your breathing down too, and *allow* the orgasmic sensations to come upon you rather than trying to make them happen.

Energy Work and Meditation

24. BEGIN AT THE END

At the very beginning of your lovemaking, take time for a short meditation in which each of you imagines how you want the lovemaking experience to unfold. First, have a brief, intimate conversation in which you reach agreement on the quality of the experience you wish to create. Then, assume a meditative posture with your feet flat on the floor, your spinal column straight, and your eyes closed. Take a few deep, relaxing breaths and imagine each moment of lovemaking unfolding exactly as you desire it to be, in as much detail as you can.

It's an incredibly powerful way to encourage your experience to be what you want, rather than arriving at some accidental outcome. You're not turning your lovemaking into a goal-oriented action here. You're using this meditative tool to orchestrate a wonderful experience. You become co-creators in sacred sexuality.

25. WHOLE LOTTA SHAKIN' GOIN' ON

To arouse your energy in preparation for extended lovemaking, turn on some wild, fast music and, for approximately ten minutes, shake every bit of your body, from your feet up to your head. Shaking is also an excellent antidote when you're in a low-energy state. You'll get a good cardiovascular workout too.

26. THYMUS TAP

Build your sexual arousal together until the man is close to ejaculation. Stop your activity then and assume the Yab Yum position with full penetration (see Day 23). The woman puts her right hand on the man's chest, in the center, two or three inches above an imaginary line connecting his nipples: that's where his thymus gland is. She rubs the spot clockwise for twenty-seven circles. Next, she taps the same spot, using the back of her left hand, twenty-seven times. He'll let her know how gently or forcefully he wants her to tap. Then he'll tap her thymus. Thymus tapping helps

- pull sexual energy up from your genitals;

- balance the left and right hemispheres of your brain;
- stimulate your immune system for optimal health.

27. ECSTASY CHANTING

At a peak of sexual arousal, stop what you are doing and become still. With the lingam still deeply inside the yoni, begin to chant together. You might start with the classic mantra "OM" or "Aum," or you can make any kind of melodious sounds you're moved to express. Harmonize your sounds and feel their vibrations, allowing yourselves to be transported into sublime states of consciousness. Sacred sounds will carry your energy up through your body and out into the cosmos. Your physical boundaries may simply dissolve as you become one with the sound, your lover, and everything.

28. MONK'S WALK

The monk's consciousness is acutely tuned to slow time. His thought is calm, his movements slow and deliberate. In this exercise, you will walk with excruciating slowness. Your attention is laser-focused on feeling first the heel of your right foot lifting off the ground, then the ball of your right foot, then your toes. Finally, your right foot is in the air, moving forward. Then the heel lightly touches down, followed by the front of the foot. In turn, your left heel ever so slowly rises off the ground, followed by the ball of the foot and your toes, and then the entire foot is in the air. Next, the left heel very lightly touches down, followed by the front of the foot, and so on for each deliberate step.

Walk together like this, paying complete attention only to your steps, for about ten minutes. Take turns leading and following. This simple exercise can bring your consciousness fully into the present moment in a most delightful way. It's a wonderful prelude to lovemaking, or you can use it as a break between sessions of intercourse. You can make every act during lovemaking a monk's walk if you focus intently and slowwwwwww wayyyyy downnnnn.

29. MASCULINE YONI, FEMININE LINGAM

In this exercise from David and Ellen Ramsdale's excellent book *Sexual Energy Ecstasy*, the woman imagines that her clitoris is a lingam and the man imagines that the urethral opening at the tip of his penis is a yoni.

Be sure that you are both in a high state of sexual arousal; then assume a comfortable position such as the Lovers' Scissors or Yab Yum. At first, the lingam rests outside the yoni, with its urethral opening close to the tip of the clitoris. The man imagines his urethra opening and expanding, like a yoni. As it opens, he allows his feminine energy to awaken. The woman imagines her clitoris engorging and enlarging, like a lingam. As it becomes erect, she allows her masculine energy to come alive.

Next, as the lingam is slowly and gently inserted into the yoni, the man imagines that he is being penetrated by his partner's penis. His imaginary yoni opens wide to receive this glorious penetration. He surrenders completely and unconditionally, allowing his goddess to take him. The woman imagines that her clitoris continues to grow larger and more erect, penetrating deeply into her lover's yoni, filling it to the limit. She takes her lover and satisfies him through and through.

This exercise sounds strange at first, but it works splendidly. Suspend your disbelief and try it. It's one of the best exercises we've used to balance our internal masculine and feminine energies. For most, it works best with closed eyes.

30. ENERGY AWAKENING WITH YOUR LOVER

Take turns being the giver and the receiver.

The Receiver

- The receiver lies naked on her back.

- Her feet are comfortably apart; her legs are flat on the bed and just far enough apart to open her genitals to the air.

- Her arms are outstretched slightly away from her sides, with palms facing up.

- Her jaw is relaxed, her mouth slightly open, and her tongue to the roof of her mouth.

- With closed eyes, she consciously relaxes her body and breathes slowly and deeply for one minute.

- She then opens her eyes and looks into the eyes of the giver.

The Giver

- The giver is sitting comfortably to her right.

- When she opens her eyes, he says words to this effect: "My goddess, it would give me great joy to awaken you to the ecstasy of energy."

- The receiver says, "Yes, thank you."

- The giver then rubs his palms briskly together for thirty seconds to build heat and energy.

- With his right hand, he gently covers her perineum and yoni and, with loving consciousness, passes energy into her. His right hand stays here throughout the meditation.

- With his left hand, he *very slowly* begins to stroke up the center of her body, from her yoni to her crown, moving the energy up with his stroking.

- His strokes are long, swooping gestures, made very lightly on the skin and done with the whole hand.

- He ends the stroke at the crown with a lifting away and above the head, then returns to the yoni.

- Both partners visualize and focus on allowing the energy to flow up through the receiver.

- To help push the energy up, the receiver gently contracts and relaxes her PC muscles in sync with the stroking. The rest of her body stays totally relaxed.

- The giver speaks words of endearment and encouragement as he strokes—for example, "Beloved, I am the awakener, charging you with my love and my life force. Accept my loving gift."

- He continues to stroke up his love's body, gradually increasing the tempo of the caress.

- Both partners continue to breathe in a slow, deep fashion.

- After six minutes, he stops his caresses and places his left hand on her heart chakra—the Sea of Tranquility.

- For one minute, the giver and the receiver gaze into each other's eyes, allowing their love to flow between them.

- The giver very slowly and gently removes his hands and lies down beside the receiver, with their bodies touching—her right side to his left.

- They both focus on the energy connection between them.

- After two minutes, the partners switch roles and continue the practice.

- They complete the meditation with a full body hug.

Sexual Play and Fantasy

31. LOVERS' MUSIC

Make a list of your lover's favorite musicians, singers, and bands. What styles of music are favored? What particular CDs are top picks? Keep the list up to date and handy. Purchase selections from your list for special occasions and surprise gifts. Play especially sensual, romantic, and spiritual songs during your lovers' time.

32. MAKING OUT À LA HIGH SCHOOL

Make out like high school virgins. Engage in a few hours of foreplay only. Don't consummate your lovemaking with intercourse or any climax of release—no ejaculation and no orgasms. You will be *sooo* hot the next day!

33. BODY KISSES

Work through the alphabet A to Z. For each letter, find a place on the body to kiss—a body part whose name begins with that letter. If you can't think of one for a particular letter, make up a name. Alternate back and forth finding places to kiss. This will get your funny bone working and creative juices flowing—not to mention other "bones" and juices!

34. POETIC HEARTS

Afterplay is what you do after sexual intercourse, and in this case it doesn't include rolling over and going to sleep. After lovingly and gently disengaging from intercourse, write a short poem in which you describe what you feel for each other. Writing a poem when you are in the transformed state after superb lovemaking—deep emotional attachment, intense pleasure and satiation, creative inspiration—can be a wondrous experience. Don't worry about how good your poetry is. All you need is a sincere sharing of what your open heart tells you to write. As you repeat this exercise several times, you'll be astonished that you're capable of communicating such sublime love and beauty. You'll come to know that love and beauty are simple, honest expressions of your true nature.

35. SPINNING WHEELS

Get naked and use washable body paints to apply spinning wheels (or other chakra symbols, such as triangles and stars within circles surrounded by lotus petals) to the seven chakras or energy points on your bodies. If you use henna instead of body paints, your designs will last for two or three weeks. Location of the chakra points, with colors indicated, are described below:

1. Perineum—red

2. Belly (above the pubic bone and below the belly button)—orange

3. Solar plexus (center of the body, below your rib cage)—yellow

4. Heart (center of chest, between the nipples)—green

5. Throat (where the man's Adam's apple is located)—blue

6. Third eye (center of the forehead)—purple

7. Crown (center of the top of the head)—white

Proceed with your lovemaking. When you're finished, wash the paint away.

36. DRESS-UPS

Wear costumes and masks during your foreplay. Change clothes several times during the course of several hours of lovemaking, choosing different outfits to establish different moods.

37. PLAYING ON THE WILD SIDE

Restrain your lover with a blindfold and tie-ups. One of the simplest and most common fantasies, and an exciting form of erotic play, it's also one of the best ways to explore unconditional surrender and complete trust. You are vulnerable and at your lover's mercy.

Use strips of silk or leather or other soft, natural fabrics. Silk scarves work perfectly, but beware not to make the ties so tight that they impair blood circulation. Specially made handcuffs, with soft linings on the cuffs to protect the tender skin of wrists and ankles, are available in most sex-toy shops.

Following are a few ideas to kick-start your imagination for teasing, tantalizing, and "torturing" your helpless victim:

- Heat a teaspoon in hot water and apply it to various parts of the body.

- Do the same with ice cubes.

- Put a spoon of honey mixed with black pepper into your mouth and then take your lover's lingam into your mouth, putting it into contact with the honey-pepper mixture.

- Dissolve a very strong mint, such as an Altoid, in your mouth, and then perform cunnilingus on your lover.

- Apply love bites and exotic scratches to your lover's willing body.

- Apply some alcohol to the nipples and then blow on them.

- Paint on your lover's body with chocolate sauce, honey, or whipped cream, and then lick it off.

38. DOCTOR FANTASY

Regular breast examinations for lumps and irregularities are essential for all women. Combine this activity with a fantasy in which your lover is a medical doctor you're consulting for a breast examination. What starts out as a legitimate breast exam turns into a forbidden, passionate encounter between doctor and patient.

First, show your man how to properly examine your breasts so he really can be on the alert for any abnormalities, but then play out the rest of the fantasy to your mutual desire. With a little imagination, you can go on to a vaginal exam, rectal exam, and so on. Start by saying, "Take off your clothes."

39. FOOD FOR GOD AND GODDESS

Prepare a meal together in various stages of undress. Interrupt the food preparation for interludes of quick, passionate lovemaking without the man going on to ejaculation. Several one- to five-minute quickies while preparing a meal can whip you up to a maddening frenzy of intense excitement.

Go on picnics. Feed each other food and drink, sometimes blindfolded. Use your fingers. Make a mess. Wear edible undies and devour them as a pre-dinner hors d'oeuvre or an after-dinner dessert.

Ritual and Ceremony

Tantrism proposes that man and God are an undivided unity (non-dual). God is everything; therefore, you—and everyone and everything else—are also God. Nothing is separate from God, because separation implies dualism. This differs from pantheism, which suggests that there is one God and everything is part of God. In Tantrism, everything is not *part* of God; everything *is* God.

Consider a hologram as an analogy to help understand this concept. Holography is a photographic method in which light from three different sources is reflected from an object onto a surface, capturing the image in three dimensions. When light is shone through that recorded image, a lifelike object appears—it may even seem as if a real person were standing before you. If you cut the original recorded image in half and shine the light through it, you still get the full image. In other words, each part of the image, however small, contains 100 percent of the whole image.

Because we are in bodily form, we perceive the world as dual and use dualistic concepts to help us understand its nature. So in Tantric practice, although everything is God, Shiva and Shakti are pictured as its masculine and feminine aspects. Shiva is fundamental, unchanging consciousness, and Shakti is the creative face of this consciousness, the energy of life. During Tantric lovemaking, lovers become the god and goddess pair Shiva and Shakti, and in their union, they reconnect with the essential Self. In a sense, you remember who you really are. Tantric rituals and ceremonies help you to transcend the limited perception of Self as a separate individual and to reunite with everything. You aren't just a two-dimensional, flat photo; you're the holographic all.

With all Tantric ceremonies and rituals, it is most important that you cultivate a state of consciousness characterized by love, adoration, and worship. You surrender to your highest Self and open to welcome an infusion of bliss as you remember that you are Shiva/Shakti. You can enhance any ceremonial practice by abstaining from sexual intercourse for one or more days beforehand. Fasting will also heighten your awareness and receptivity to the cosmic energy. The longer your preparation period of sexual abstinence and fasting, the more intense your ritual will be. Historically, Tantric practitioners also use intoxicating substances to enhance their experience. They also employ earthly materials in their rituals as symbols of divine qualities.

Tantric rituals generally involve the preparation of a sacred space, bathing, relaxing the body, clearing the mind with meditation and deep breathing, sending out evil and inviting in love, focusing on the ultimate purpose of the ritual (union with Shiva/Shakti), and giving thanks to each other for honoring god and goddess in this manner.

40. TANTRIC RITUAL 1: I AM THAT

In Tantra, Shiva is the pure witness consciousness, that out of which all existence comes and to which all existence eventually returns. Shakti is the manifestation of physical reality out of pure consciousness. "THAT" refers to the various objects (trees, rocks, water) of physical reality that make up the universe, as well as the subjects, including you and all other human beings—each with a seemingly isolated awareness of existence. When you repeat the mantra "I AM THAT," you are giving recognition to the unity of this trinity—Shiva (I), Shakti (AM), and yourself (THAT). By repeating this mantra, you establish your intention to wake up and return to God consciousness. How many times do you have to repeat the mantra? A student asked his guru how many lifetimes he would have to go on practicing. His guru replied, "Seventy thousand." The student exclaimed in joy, "Only seventy thousand?!" And at that moment, he became enlightened.

41. TANTRIC RITUAL 2: TRICAPETA[1] (THE THREE TAPS)

This simple ritual symbolically honors and gives recognition to the cycle of unity/duality/unity, or birth/life/death. Our individual consciousness emerges from cosmic consciousness (birth), exists to enjoy a short visit in the dualism of time and space with awareness of all the pairs of opposites (life), and then returns to the eternal oneness (death).

Sit comfortably. Relax your body. Calm your mind.

The First Tap

The first tap is to the feet. As you tap each foot, say aloud the affirmation, "My body is the entire universe. I am my body. My body is freedom." Your feet are closest to the earth—material reality, the grossest aspect of consciousness manifested as form. They are the means of moving from one location to another, symbolizing your movement from a contracted individual consciousness to a more expanded cosmic consciousness.

The Second Tap

The second tap is from one hand to the other hand. As you tap each hand, say aloud the affirmation, "I am my mind, thought, perception, and the very process of knowing all things. My mind is freedom." Your hands symbolize that which takes and shapes material reality into useful forms, while realizing that all forms are ephemeral and short-lived, eventually dissolving back into Ultimate Reality.

The Third Tap

The third tap is to the top of the head, the crown chakra. As you tap your head, say aloud the affirmation, "I am the knower, the witness, the creator before time and space, within time and space, after time and space. I am God and Goddess, all and everything, the one without a second. I am my Soul. My Soul is freedom." The crown chakra is your bridge that unites the material world of dualism with the non-dual world of pure consciousness.

42. TANTRIC RITUAL 3: HONORING YONI AND LINGAM

Take turns gazing at each other's genitals. One of you sits on a chair with your legs spread apart, exposing your genitals to view. Your lover sits on the floor directly in front of you.

A man gazing at his lover's yoni repeats these words, either out loud or as a silent thought: "This yoni is the great goddess Shakti in the flesh—source of all life, all healing, and my liberation from illusion, confusion, and suffering. She is the source of sublime pleasure and all good things."

A woman gazing at her lover's lingam repeats these words, either out loud or as a silent thought: "This lingam is Shiva in the flesh—the wand of light, seed of life, and my liberation from illusion, confusion, and suffering. He is the source of sublime pleasure and all good things."

Look for twenty minutes, or as long as an hour, and repeat the words over and over. You are honoring the lingam and yoni as symbols of the merging of the universal masculine and feminine energies, returning you to your divine origin: cosmic consciousness.

43. TANTRIC RITUAL 4: OUTER SPACE/ INNER SPACE

In this simple ceremony, you give recognition to the ten directions: east, southeast, south, southwest, west, northwest, north, northeast, horizon (below), and heavens (above). By naming and honoring the ten directions, you claim their properties as personal powers and are liberated from all constraints of space as a limited locality. You claim your freedom to move anywhere on the planet while in your body, and also to travel as pure consciousness outside of your body, beyond time and space. As you expand in all directions simultaneously, you realize your identity with infinite space.

In spiritual practice, it is assumed that whatever direction you are facing is always east. This is significant, because it affirms that your essential Self transcends the physical geographic limitations of the directions on a compass. If you do know the compass direction of east, face that direction for this practice, but if not, face any direction you choose—for example, the one with the best view, such as off the edge of a cliff, across a body of water, or out of a large window. Facing east, south is to your right and north is to your left.

To begin, face east, snap the fingers of both hands, and chant "OM" three times. Turning in a clockwise direction (toward south), repeat the snapping and chanting at each direction. For horizon, look down toward the earth, and for heavens, glance up toward the sky. Finish with heavens.

44. TANTRIC RITUAL 5: HOLY WATER

Place a glass or a crystal container of water in direct sunlight for a full day to remove all energetic contaminants.

Bless the water in the following way. Touch the thumb and middle finger of each hand together to form a circle, and touch both circles together. You'll make a shape symbolic of infinity (transcends space) and eternity (transcends time). Stand facing each other, and put your two infinity symbols together over the purified water. These hand actions are sacred *mudras* (ritualized body movements). Chant the "OM" mantra together twenty-seven times.

This blessed water can now be used for ceremonial practices. For example:

• Sprinkle some around the room, upon your bed, your altar, or the food you will consume, blessing everything you'll see and use during your sacred sexual loving.

• Sprinkle some at the threshold of each doorway into your home for protection against unwelcome entities, energies, or spirits.

45. TANTRIC RITUAL 6: FIVE OFFERINGS

The essence of the physical universe is contained within these five principles: ether (space), air, fire, water, and earth. In this ritual, you utilize the five elements to honor the yoni and lingam, symbols of Shakti and Shiva. By doing so, you reclaim the powers of the five elements, balance your masculine and feminine energies, and return to God consciousness, in which you know "I AM THAT."

Gather together these properties: flowers for ether, incense or sweet grass for air, a candle for fire, your blessed water for water, and moist modeling clay or wet soil for earth.

Honoring the Yoni

- The woman lies naked.

- Her lover lights the candle and sets it between her legs, near her yoni.

- He gently and reverently rubs some of the wet clay onto her outer vaginal lips.

- Slowly, he lays the flowers and sprinkles the holy water onto her yoni.

- He lights the incense or sweet grass—the smudge.

- Holding the candle in his left hand and the smudge in his right hand above the yoni, he moves the candle in a clockwise direction and the smudge in a counterclockwise direction three times. This motion creates the infinity symbol and draws consciousness back to its divine origins—"I AM THAT."

- While moving the candle and smudge, he repeats these words, one sentence for each of the three circles:

  - "I honor your yoni."

  - "I surrender to your yoni."

  - "When I enter this sacred cave, I awaken to become one with Goddess."

Honoring the Lingam

- The man lies naked.

- His lover lights the candle and sets it between his legs, near his lingam.

- She lovingly rubs some of the wet clay onto the shaft of his penis.

- She sprinkles the flowers and holy water onto it.

- She lights the incense or sweet grass.

- Holding the candle in her left hand and the smudge in her right hand above the penis, she moves the candle in a clockwise direction and the smudge in a counterclockwise direction three times. This motion creates the infinity symbol and draws consciousness back to its divine origins—"I AM THAT." While moving the candle and smudge, she repeats these words, one sentence for each of the three circles:

- "I honor your lingam."
- "I surrender to your lingam."
- "When your lingam enters my sacred cave, I awaken to become one with God."

46. TANTRIC RITUAL 7: YONI AND LINGAM PUJA

In Sanskrit, *puja* means "offering, honoring, worship, meditation, ceremony, or ritual." In this ritual, you once again work with the five elements of Indian cosmology: ether (space), air, fire, water, and earth. You will pour these five liquids over your genitals:

- ether: edible cooking oil
- air: milk
- fire: honey
- water: your blessed water
- earth: yogurt

As the fluids come into contact with the sacred yoni and lingam, they are purified, energized, and blessed. When you consume it, this mixture beckons you to enter into the sacred, mysterious realm of cosmic consciousness, in which you realize that you are not separate from Shiva and Shakti, but rather that you *are* Shiva and Shakti. According to the *Upanishads* (*Mahanarayanopanisad*), "By this oblation may my mind, speech, sight, hearing, taste, smell, seed, intellect, intention, and aim become purified. May my seven bodily ingredients—outer and inner skin, flesh, blood, fat, marrow, sinew, and bone—become purified. By this oblation may the qualities of sound, touch, sight, taste, and smell, residing in the five elements constituting my body, become purified."[2]

- Naked, lie down or sit in a position that makes it easy for your lover to capture the fluid mixture as it drips off your genitals. Use a small bowl or decorative cup to catch it.

- One at a time, apply each fluid to your genitals and, as you do, say, "I am ether," "I am air," "I am fire," and so on.

- After gathering the mixtures, each of you will drink one-half of the yoni elixir and one-half of the lingam elixir.

- As you drink, speak aloud three times, "I AM THAT," while holding in your consciousness that you are Shiva/Shakti.

For a powerful variation, add your genital secretions to the elixir—semen, urine, menstrual blood, and female ejaculate. In the Tantric tradition, these fluids are sacred and highly charged with vital spiritual life force. Consuming them infuses your being with energy and awakens the highest consciousness. According to the *Chandamaharosana Tantra*: "Eat my essence! Drink the Waters of Release! This is the best diet, eaten by all Buddhas."[3]

47. TANTRIC RITUAL 8: EMPTINESS IS FULLNESS, FULLNESS IS LIFE

Wood ashes symbolize the emptiness left after fire has burned away all impurities and all ego-centeredness, leaving only pure Shiva consciousness. Menstrual blood is symbolic of the generative power of the life force—Shakti energy—in creating manifest reality. Perform this ritual as follows:

- Smear white ashes all over your bodies.
- Mark the top of your feet, your pubic mound, your navel just below your belly button, your solar plexus, your heart center, your throat, your third eye, and the top of your head with drops of menstrual blood.
- Mix three drops of menstrual blood and three pinches of wood ashes in a glass of your holy water.
- Build your sexual arousal to an orgasmic peak, but stop before the climax.
- Take three sips from your sacred elixir and then pour one-half of the remaining liquid over each of your heads.
- Together, speak aloud 108 times the mantra "I AM THAT."
- Resume sexual intercourse and, at climax, both speak out loud, "I AM THAT," three times.

48. TANTRIC RITUAL 9: CEREMONY OF SURRENDER

In this ceremony, the man will completely surrender to his goddess. According to the Buddhist *Hevajra Tantra*: "At all times, whether washing one's feet or eating, rinsing the mouth, rubbing the hands, girding the hips with a loincloth, going out, making conversation, walking, standing, in wrath, in laughter; the wise man should always worship and honor the lady."[4]

The first night, he is allowed to sleep in the same room, but only on the floor beside her bed. He may retire only after having lovingly washed and perfumed his goddess's feet. The second night, he can sleep in the bed with her, but he must be fully clothed. The third night, he may sleep naked beside her, but without touching her. The fourth night, he may kiss, fondle, and caress her, but he cannot touch the yoni. The fifth night, he may pleasure the yoni orally, but he may not enter the sacred place. The sixth night, he may penetrate the yoni with his lingam, but he may not ejaculate. The seventh night, he may ejaculate if he so chooses, or he may voluntarily retain his seed. According to the *Chandamaharosana Tantra*: "I (Shakti) am identical to the bodies of all women and there is no way that I can be worshipped except by the worship of women. Visualizing that she is fully my embodiment, he should make love to his woman. Because of uniting the vajra (lingam) and padma (yoni), I will grant enlightenment."[5]

49. TANTRIC RITUAL 10: GRAND RITUAL OF TANTRA

According to the *Kamakhya Tantra*: "The true devotee should worship the Mother of the Universe with liquor, fish, meat, cereal, and copulation."[6] These are often referred to as the five Ms: *madya* (wine or other alcohol), *matsya* (fish), *mamsa* (meat), *mudra* (various cereal grains, often mixed with cannabis), and *maithuna* (a mixture of genital secretions; for example, menstrual blood and semen). Right-hand (celibate) practitioners of Tantra substitute the following ingredients for the five Ms: coconut milk, cheese, ginger, rice, and honey.

The Grand Ritual of Tantra[7] in Sanskrit is *pancamakara* (five observances). In the West, the term *maithuna* is now commonly used as synonymous with *pancamakara*, referring to the entire practice, not just the genital secretion mixture. Historically, pancamakara was often celebrated by groups of lovers. Sumerians had a similar practice called *Hieros Gamos* (from the Greek), referring to sacred coupling. There is a Hieros Gamos scene in Stanley Kubrick's movie *Eyes Wide Shut*, and the practice is mentioned in Dan Brown's novel *The Da Vinci Code*. In Wicca, there is a similar ceremony called the Great Rite.

Pancamakara refers to practices of sacramental intercourse—the meditation of sex. It's an elaborate Tantric ritual with many parts, culminating in some form of sacred sexual union in which man and woman unite as one. As with all Tantric rituals, your intention is to awaken the realization that you are Shiva/Shakti, the divine one without a second. You intentionally stimulate all your mental faculties and physical senses to the maximum, reclaiming that life-force energy for spiritual awakening. Or, as Philip Rawson declares, "Raise your enjoyment to its highest power, and then use it as a spiritual rocket fuel."[8]

In this ritual, by denying yourself the release of ejaculatory orgasm, you awaken the kundalini energy lying dormant at your coccyx so that it may rise up your spinal column, entering your brain with a rush of bliss consciousness. According to Gopi Krishna[9]: "The ambrosia is the nectarlike reproductive secretion which, at the highest point of ecstasy, pours into the brain with such an intensely pleasurable sensation that even the sexual orgasm pales into insignificance before it. This unbelievably rapturous sensation—pervading the whole of the spinal cord, the organs of generation and the brain—is

nature's incentive to the effort directed at self-transcendence, as the orgasm is the incentive to the reproductive act."

Of the five Ms, madya may include various forms of alcohol, as well as other intoxicants and aphrodisiacs. Wine, beer, or spirits are examples of alcohol. Other intoxicants could include cannabis (marijuana or hashish). With intoxicants, more is not better: moderation is best. For aphrodisiacs, we suggest ingesting several drops of alcohol-based tinctures of Damiana and Muira Puama. If you use this aphrodisiac daily in "Tantric Ritual 9: Ceremony of Surrender," you'll have made an extraordinary preparation for the pancamakara ritual.

Here are the basic steps for the Grand Ritual of Tantra (pancamakara):

1. Honoring the god and goddess by asking permission to join each other in union

2. Tantric Ritual 1: "I AM THAT" (combine mantra with harmonized breathing and eye gazing)

3. Create sacred space (a form of mandala)

4. Tantric Ritual 4: Outer Space/Inner Space

5. Sacred bathing (a form of mudra)

6. Tantric Ritual 2: Tricapeta (The Three Taps)

7. Tantric Ritual 6: Five Offerings (honoring yoni and lingam deities)

8. Erotic massage (includes internal prostate massage)

9. Sacramental intercourse (various peaks, with Yab Yum and Scissors positions)

10. The five Ms (share wine, food, and genital secretions over a period of hours together)

11. Tantric Ritual 7: Yoni and Lingam Puja

12. Thank you

50. SEXUAL MAGIC

As you approach and then experience orgasmic climax, create a clear image in your consciousness of an outcome that is your heart's desire. Imagine the chakra center at the middle of your forehead (your third eye) opening, and visualize a projectile of pure energy carrying your image into the blackness of space. See the projectile burst open, with bits of colored light spreading out in all directions at once—for instance, the seven chakra colors of red, orange, yellow, green, blue, purple, and white. All possibilities exist within infinite space. You are identical with that space. Your very Self is space. Of course, you can create what you truly want, because "I AM THAT."

The power of this sexual magic is dramatically enhanced when you both project the same vision at the same instant. Work with only one desire at any particular session of lovemaking.

SIX

Continuing Your Practice

You've completed your wondrous twenty-eight-day journey together. Build on what you've worked so hard to accomplish by continuing your practice. In this chapter, we give you suggestions for daily activities as well as recommendations for weekly, monthly, and yearly connection. Keep your relationship thriving, passionate, and spiritually fresh for years to come.

Daily

In the twenty-eight-day plan, you undertook your practice with a daily twenty-minute session together. We encourage you to continue practicing together, but if you want to progress more rapidly, you can also add Tantric exercises to do by yourself throughout the day. Also, sometimes you will be apart from each other for several days, even weeks, so below

we outline three possible practice patterns. First, there's practicing only together. Next, there are suggestions for activities to do both with your partner and by yourself. Third are practices to do on your own when you are apart.

1. PRACTICING TOGETHER ONLY

- Continuing with a twenty-minute daily connection will exponentially increase the intimacy of your relationship.

- If you can't do twenty minutes together every day, try every second day or three or more times per week.

- Highly recommended to include are
  - PC pumping (try different variations);
  - looks of love;
  - body scan and grounding;

- conscious breath and meditation—choose one from the twenty-eight-day plan or from this chapter.

- You can repeat any of the days from the twenty-eight-day plan.

- You can add new activities from this chapter.

2. PRACTICING TOGETHER AND ON YOUR OWN

Do some activities on your own at various times during the day, and do some activities together. We highly recommend you include these:

- *Body Scan and Grounding:* You can continue this together and also start adding it throughout the day, as often as you remember to do it. Eventually, you can be grounded all the time, even while you're doing other complex activities.

- *PC Pumping:* Fifty squeezes. Do them with your partner during combination breath and meditation practices, or spread them throughout the day on your own—for instance, while sitting, driving, or waiting.

- *Looks of Love:* Do this exercise for two minutes together.

- Other activities described in this chapter, such as

  - *Loving Laughter:* two minutes, alone or together;

  - *Sudden Flash of Bliss Meditation:* five minutes, alone or together;

  - *Lovers' Scissors Meditation:* five minutes to connect most intimately, if you have the luxury of waking up together in the morning or going to sleep together at night.

The one to five minutes each of these practices takes is time even the busiest people can fit into their demanding schedules. No extra time is required for grounding and PC pumping; you can do them while you're doing other things. The other four practices listed can be done in a total of fifteen minutes. You can fit the looks of love, loving laughter, and meditation practices anywhere into your day. For example, you could do the looks of love when you first meet after returning from work, loving laughter just before dinner, and the Lovers' Scissors and the bliss meditation when you first wake up in the morning. The real challenge is not finding the time but remembering to do the practices. Create some way to help you remember—for example, Post-it notes stuck where you'll see them, a string around your wrist, reminders on your computer, and so on.

3. WHEN YOU'RE APART—EXERCISES TO DO ON YOUR OWN

- Almost no couple is together every day of the year. You can continue your practice when you're apart, even when it's for considerable lengths of time. Then, when you're back together again, you'll be charged up for each other.

- Highly recommended are
  - body scan and grounding;
  - PC pumping (fifty per day);
  - one of the breath and meditation practices from the twenty-eight days or from this chapter;
  - anything else that appeals to you—for instance, the "You're Perfect" practice found in this chapter.

Weekly

HIGHLY RECOMMENDED

- Extended lovemaking session (minimum one hour, preferably four hours or more)

- Internal prostate massage

One of the main challenges for creating a weekly lovers' time is making arrangements for child care. One creative solution is to trade kids with another couple, so both couples can have time alone. Other family members may be available to watch over your children. And there's always the paid babysitting option.

Monthly

HIGHLY RECOMMENDED

- A full thirty minutes of one-minute PC squeezes. See the advanced PC pumping exercises for men and women in this chapter.

- A lovers' weekend away from home, family, and work. At least once or twice per year should be possible for most couples, if they really want to do this. Why not make it a learning weekend, during which you attend a relationship or sacred sexuality workshop?

Annually

HIGHLY RECOMMENDED

- Renew your vows of commitment.

- Repeat the full twenty-eight-day plan for Tantric ecstasy.

- Take a one-week lovers' holiday, just the two of you. Disengage from all of life's responsibilities, especially work and kids. Imagine being disconnected from your cell phone, handheld PDA, and computer for a whole week.

Optional Selections

Pick from these options as frequently as you desire, adding them into your daily, weekly, or monthly lovers' practice.

- Relationship and Communication
- Breathing
- Meditation
- Energy Circulation and Exchange
- Sexual Fitness

RELATIONSHIP AND COMMUNICATION

Removing Blocks

When you have an issue with your lover, it can sabotage your lovemaking. Sometimes, negative feelings can be so strong that you don't want to make love at all. First, write a letter to your partner explaining the situation as objectively and fairly as you can. Second, write a letter as if it were the response you want to receive from your lover. Share both letters with your partner and open a dialogue about how to address the issue.

Get Ready for Love

Plan and prepare for your extended lovemaking sessions with the same investment of time and energy you'd put into preparing for a business presentation, a course assignment at a university, or an artistic performance onstage.

- Creating a sacred space is something we recommend you do every time you have an extended lovemaking session. Gather together a collection of items for use in creating your lovers' space and keep them handy so that you have what you want when you want it.

- Research information on interesting conversation topics, particularly something you know your partner will find engaging. Stretch yourself by going outside your comfort zone—for example, by selecting a topic that's completely new to you.

- Prepare questions to ask your lover during your playtime, especially after intercourse.

- Select clothing or costumes you can wear over the course of your hours together—for example, sexy lingerie, bathrobes, dinner dress, and erotic, casual, and fantasy outfits for role playing.

- Have a selection of sex toys available. Check your batteries.

- Gather music suitable for different moods—for example, slow dancing, fast dancing, mystical mood music, sexy lovemaking music, and heart-opening romantic ballads.

- Collect erotic poetry or short stories to read to your lover, or find books of erotic photography you can browse through together.

- Organize a selection of other properties to choose from when the mood suggests they'd fit. Here are some examples:

  - Sensual bath soaps, bubbles, and salts
  - Essential oils and diffuser
  - Massage oils
  - Water or silicone lubricants
  - Candles
  - Beautiful fabric remnants (red, purple, and gold) to drape over sharp edges
  - Washable body paints
  - Incense or sweet grass for smudging
  - Bottled water, mineral water, or club soda
  - Champagne or wine with suitable glassware
  - Healthy snacks and fresh, light, nutritious food for lunch or dinner
  - Gourmet coffee or tea
  - Fresh fruit
  - Dark chocolate
  - Musical instruments
  - Ceremonial objects, such as a Tibetan singing bowl
  - A collection of masks, tie-ups, and other items for exotic play

- The best towels and bed linens you can afford
- Fresh-cut flowers and a selection of houseplants
- Safe-sex items, such as condoms, dental dams, and latex gloves or finger cots

Relationship as Spiritual Practice

Most of our psychological and emotional "stuff" comes up in the context of intimate relationships. Use this natural, universal condition to help you heal and mature. Take turns revealing to each other how highly emotional issues in your relationship have enabled you to grow and awaken spiritually.

For example, disagreements over money may have brought into your awareness that you've been carrying a poverty consciousness with you from early childhood. Now that you've faced it, you are able to begin creating abundance on all levels. Or, you may discover how avoiding sexual intimacy is connected to an early experience of sexual abuse. This awareness clears the way for a profound inner healing, opening you to experience the wonder of sexual ecstasy.

Becoming aware of how your relationship has helped you heal in the past can provide a powerful motivation to continue using it as one of your most important spiritual assets. Look for issues about which you disagree most strongly and argue most frequently. Every one is a doorway opening for you to reclaim your spiritual freedom. Instead of fighting with each other over your differences, use that energy to transcend your current limits and help each other become whole.

Renewing Vows of Commitment

If you're in a committed long-term relationship, renew your vows every year. Do it privately, or invite witnesses. In your ceremony, communicate all the ways you want, need, and love your partner. Add in any promises that you intend to honor, perhaps about fidelity or spending time together. Many of us have experienced the breaking of vows, so it's unrealistic to assume that vows once spoken will last for life. By renewing them yearly, you confirm that your commitment remains strong. It also gives you the opportunity to update your vows so that they accurately and honestly convey how you feel about each other now. Consummate your vows with the most passionate lovemaking.

Just Because

Once per month, surprise each other with a special gift: one that you purchase or one that you make. If you like, wrap it beautifully for presentation to your beloved. As you offer your gift, make it clear that you're giving it only because you love and wish to honor your partner. Your mate deserves all good things. You expect absolutely nothing in return. It's simply your way of saying, "I love you just because you are you, because you are here with me, and I am ever so grateful for that."

BREATHING

Ten Breaths to the Center of the Cyclone

Take a slow, deep breath, just until you're comfortably full of air. As soon as you're full of air, exhale slowly. Inhale and exhale at the same rate, without any pause between. Establish a slow, deliberate breathing rhythm.

Now, start counting your breaths. Count each breath on the exhale. Count to ten breaths. Start over again at one. Counting on the exhale helps you focus. Counting to ten and then starting over at one is an attention check. If you find yourself at fifteen or twenty-one, you know your attention has wandered. Don't make it a big deal or berate yourself. Give yourself a mental hug for noticing your meandering mind, and gently resume your breath count from one again.

At first, getting to ten without losing your focus will be a significant achievement. With practice over a period of weeks, you should be able to get to a count of ten, perhaps ten to thirty times. When you're able to do this, you will have trained your thought process to keep your attention focused on whatever you want for an extended period of time. Attention in the now moment during lovemaking is one of the core competencies of Tantric sex.

Hyperdrive Breathing

As you become sexually aroused, you naturally breathe rapidly. You can also deliberately use rapid breath to build your excitement, energy, and arousal. Many stage performers use this method to prepare for shows.

Do the hyperdrive breath through your mouth. Inhale and exhale rapidly and forcefully. You're saturating all your body's cells with a rich supply of oxygen. Do this breath for about one minute and you'll likely feel a bit lightheaded (hyperventilated), but not dangerously so. If you're too dizzy, reduce the number of rapid breaths until you find your comfort zone.

Twenty to sixty seconds of the hyperdrive breath readies you for peak performance, whether in bed, onstage, or in a competition.

Yin/Yang Breath
The yin/yang breath balances your inner masculine and feminine energies. It awakens and balances your left and right brain centers, giving you both mental clarity and mystical sensitivity. Perhaps you've noticed that during the day your body routinely shifts breathing from nostril to nostril. Sometimes you breathe primarily through the left nostril, stimulating the right brain. Other times you breathe primarily through the right nostril, stimulating the left brain. At night, in bed, when you lie on your right side, you breathe primarily through your left nostril. When you turn onto your left side, you breathe through the right.

With yin/yang breathing, you deliberately breathe through one nostril at a time. Start by gently squeezing your nose between your thumb and the ring and little fingers of one hand. Remove your thumb, but keep your fingers pressed against the other nostril. Inhale slowly through the open nostril, completely filling your lungs. Return your thumb to block that nostril, and hold for a brief mo-ment. Remove your fingers to open the other nostril, and exhale completely. Inhale through that same nostril, and then replace your fingers, blocking it. Hold. Remove your thumb, and exhale through the open nostril. Inhale through the thumb nostril, and then close it with your thumb. Hold. Remove your fingers and exhale, and so on. Repeat for five complete cycles.

MEDITATION
Loving Laughter
Laugh out loud for two minutes a day. Mary Kay's advice "Fake it till you make it" fits perfectly here. Simply start laughing and don't stop for two minutes.

You'll get quite a little physical workout. You'll release stress and tension and send lots of healthy, feel-good endorphins throughout your system. Stop after two minutes and scan your body. Do you feel lighter, better, happier?

Research shows that your brain and central nervous system can't tell the difference between an imaginary or fake experience and a real one, so the healing benefits of this laughter are equal to genuine spontaneous laughter.

Sudden Flash of Bliss

This is a core meditation from Tantrism. In spite of its utter simplicity, it can be frustratingly difficult, because the active mind refuses to settle down and becomes very impatient with any apparent lack of progress. But when it works, an epiphany of high consciousness comes to you in a flash.

- Sit in the traditional meditation pose, with legs crossed and spinal column straight.

- If possible, sit facing a blank (preferably white) wall.

- Hold your hands in the cupped-palms mudra—resting in your lap, palms facing up, with the right hand on top of the left.

- Your breath is slow and deep.

- Your eyes are open. Your gaze is soft.

- You are simply the witness. There is no need to do anything else. As thoughts float into your consciousness, simply let them be. You do not become attached to them, nor do you resist having them. Just notice them in your witness consciousness.

- You may become aware through your peripheral vision of indistinct or blurred images out of the corners of your eyes. The white wall and your peripheral vision will help your mind become still. This is easier than looking into a busy room or landscape.

Embrace Your Desires

- Sit in the standard meditation position, with legs crossed and back straight.

- Breathe slowly and deeply.

- You are the witness, becoming aware of a desire.

- Focus your attention on that desire, with the awareness that your desire is simply a manifestation of Shiva himself. There's nothing to be done with your desire. Don't accept it; don't reject it. There's no need to act upon it. Just remain as the witness, always keeping in mind that you are Shiva, watching Shiva, creating Shiva.

- Any emotions that arise, positive and negative, are simply energy taking form. You're literally creating the universe as you sit meditating.

- Allow that energy to be. Don't try to do anything with it. Don't try to deny it, avoid it, or suppress it. Just continue to be the witness.

- As you embrace your desires and the emotions associated with them as pure energy, they lose all power over you. You become free. The energy then acts to expand your consciousness.

You're Perfect

Because everything is God, everything is perfect. But we don't get that message most of the time. We're taught to continually judge and constantly seek to change and improve things, particularly ourselves. Help yourself realize your magnificence and your simple perfection with this practice.

Whenever you see yourself in a mirror, look deep into your eyes and say, "I am perfect as I am."

ENERGY CIRCULATION AND EXCHANGE

Good Morning, Lovers—The Lovers' Scissors

Get the TV out of the bedroom. Sleep naked together. Cuddle all night long like spoons; double beds, not queens or kings, are better for staying close. When you wake in the morning, connect for five minutes in the Lovers' Scissors position. Remain still, make eye contact, and breathe in harmony. Know that one person loves you completely and unconditionally, and then start your day ready for anything the world may send your way. This intimate emotional connection and sharing of energy makes an excellent daily practice. You can do it at night if you prefer.

Clearing Toxic Energy Entities

It can be helpful to imagine that negative emotions or undesirable states of consciousness take the form of an entity with a visible energy body.

- Pick any one to work with, and identify it by giving it a name—for instance, fear, shame, guilt, insecurity, and so forth.

- Notice where you most strongly feel the presence of this entity inside your body, such as tightness in your belly, stiffness in your neck, pain in your groin, an ache in your heart, nausea in your stomach, or trembling in your hands.

- Invite the entity out, so you can see it and have a conversation with it.

- Visualize it sitting across from you.

- Ask the entity what it wants from you.

- Ask yourself, "Is there any reason why I might have invited this entity to be with me? Is there some benefit I derive from being afraid, ashamed, feeling guilty, or insecure?"

- Ask yourself if there's any other way you can get the same benefit, but in a positive way.

- Once you've identified how you can do that, command the entity to leave you and never return. Make it perfectly and forcefully clear that you have no further use for its services, that it is no longer welcome inside you.

- Finally, as you repeat the mantra "I AM THAT" 108 times, know that you are forever free of that entity.

SEXUAL FITNESS

Advanced PC Pumping—Genital Awareness, Toning, Strength, and Enhanced Pleasure

You've already been working with PC pumping in your twenty-eight-day plan. The following exercises refine your practice. Doing them regularly greatly enhances your genital awareness and tones and strengthens individual muscles. You'll significantly enhance your sexual experience. Men will get and maintain erections more easily and delay ejaculation more readily. Women will increase their orgasmic pleasure.

For Men. Try to become aware and sensitive to the following: scrotum sac (testicles), penis, perineum, anus, and right and left buttocks.

- First, tighten your entire genital region by squeezing all the muscles in the area at the same time.

  - Squeeze the urethral sphincter as if you were stopping the flow of urine in midstream. It feels like you're trying to suck your penis into your body.

  - Squeeze the two anal sphincters, one at the anal rim and the other deeper inside, as if you were holding back from an urgent bowel movement or retaining an enema.

  - Raise your pelvic floor by pulling up on your perineum, tightening the coccygeus, and lifting the levator ani muscles. When you are sufficiently contracted, your buttocks will tighten.

- Don't worry if you can't identify the exact internal location of each muscle;

simply tighten everything. Later you'll gain more sensitivity and mastery and will be able to contract one muscle at a time.

- Squeeze, and hold the squeeze for approximately one minute. Relax for a few seconds and repeat this action as many as one hundred times. We strongly recommend at least fifteen or twenty repetitions. Build up to a hundred repetitions over a period of months. Don't try to do a hundred the first day. Also, you don't have to do the squeezes all at once. Spread them out throughout the day. Once you're able to do a hundred repetitions, you can maintain your sexual fitness with thirty to forty repetitions of full one-minute squeezes three or four times per week. Perhaps once or twice per month, complete the full hundred repetitions all at once.

- Learn to isolate one muscle from the others. Attempt to contract only that one muscle while keeping all the others in a state of relaxation. It can help if you're standing naked in front of a mirror. Following is a suggested sequence of practice:

1. Pull your testicles up close to your body.
2. Lift your penis, bobbing it up and down.
3. Tighten your right buttock.
4. Tighten your left buttock.
5. Tighten your anus (both anal sphincters).
6. Pull up on your perineum.
7. As you advance in your practice, add weight to your erect penis—for example by adding a washcloth, a wet washcloth, a hand towel, and then a bath towel.

For Women. In your practice, try to become aware and sensitive to the following: muscles around your urethra, vaginal canal, perineum, and anus.

- First, tighten your entire genital region by squeezing all the muscles in the area at the same time.
  - Squeeze the urethral sphincter as if you were stopping the flow of urine in midstream.
  - Contract all the muscles within your vaginal canal.

- Squeeze the two anal sphincters, one at the anal rim and the other deeper inside, as if you were holding back from an urgent bowel movement or retaining an enema.
- Raise your pelvic floor by pulling up on your perineum and tightening your coccygeus.

• Don't worry if you can't identify the exact internal location of each muscle; simply tighten everything. Later you'll gain more sensitivity and mastery and will be able to contract one muscle at a time.

• Squeeze, and hold the squeeze for approximately one minute. Relax for a few seconds and repeat this action as many as one hundred times. We strongly recommend at least fifteen or twenty repetitions. Build up to a hundred repetitions over a period of months. Don't try to do a hundred the first day. Also, you don't have to do the squeezes all at once. Spread them out throughout the day. Once you're able to do a hundred repetitions, you can maintain your sexual fitness with thirty to forty repetitions of full one-minute squeezes, three or four times per week. Perhaps once or twice per month, complete the full hundred repetitions all at once.

• Learn to isolate one muscle from the others. Attempt to contract only that one muscle while keeping all the others in a state of relaxation. Following is a suggested sequence of practice:

1. Urethra
2. Vaginal canal—start at the cervix and contract each muscle all the way to the vaginal opening
3. Perineum
4. Anus
5. Keep all the muscles flexed
6. Relax in the reverse order—from anus to perineum, then to vaginal opening and back to cervix, then to urethra
7. For advanced practice, you might try a vaginal exerciser, such as Shawna Morrisette's Oni Eggs or Betty Dodson's barbells

Abdominal Lift

You can do this exercise standing or kneeling on all fours. It provides a stimulating massage to all the organs in your abdominal cavity. Performing these movements during lovemaking, either sitting, lying down, or on your hands and knees, helps circulate sexual energy up through your body.

Standing

- Stand with your feet shoulder-width apart. Bend your legs a little at your knees.

- Lean slightly forward, placing your hands on your thighs.

- Strongly contract your abdomen, forcing all air out of your lungs.

- Raise your rib cage upward as far as possible.

- Hold for as long as it's comfortable.

- Relax your abdomen and inhale a complete breath.

- Repeat five times to start, working up to twenty-five or more over a period of several weeks.

Hands and Knees

- Kneel on your hands and knees. Put your hands directly beneath your shoulders, and keep your arms straight. Your knees are directly beneath your hips, and your feet point straight behind you. Your back is straight.

- Strongly contract your abdomen, forcing all air out of your lungs.

- Raise your rib cage upward as far as possible.

- Hold for as long as it's comfortable.

- Relax your abdomen and inhale a complete breath.

- Repeat five times to start, working up to twenty-five or more over a period of several weeks.

Also try this variation: Rapidly contract your abdominal muscles, forcing the air out through your nose. Your mouth is closed. As you relax your abdominal muscles, the air will rush back into your lungs. Pump your abdomen rapidly in this way as many times as you can, just until you begin to tire. Don't strain yourself.

Cat Stretch

If you're on your hands and knees for the abdominal lift, end by arching your back down toward the floor while at the same time turning your head up toward the ceiling. Then hump your back toward the ceiling while bringing your chin into your body. Repeat this cat stretch ten or fifteen times. You can also do the cat stretch without the abdominal lift.

SEVEN

The Essentials, Plus More Positions for Energy Exchange

The Bare Essentials

Learning the art of sacred sexuality is intended to be a joyous celebration, not a tedious task. Let your learning be as light as possible. Be gracious and kind with each other as you try new things. Remember to laugh at your challenges while rejoicing in your triumphs.

Developing skill in the art of spiritual sexuality requires many repetitions. We have intentionally built some repetition into the twenty-eight-day plan of exercises, particularly for those actions that build core sacred sex skills, such as methods of breathing, muscle contractions, visualization, focused attention, and emotional heart connection.

For most lovers, their knowledge will far exceed their skill by the end of their first full sequence together. Becoming frustrated when your knowledge increases faster than your skill will only slow your learning progress, while actually practicing the skills will speed you along your joyous learning path. Eventually you'll reach the level of mastery.

This is a workbook for couples. So if you have simply read or scanned the book without doing the recommended exercises daily, your next step is to start the twenty-eight-day plan of activities together. The most important step is to begin doing the exercises *now*, beginning with Day 1! The next most important step is to continue your practice in spite of any frustration you may experience along the way.

We recommend that you start at Day 1 and proceed through the entire twenty-eight days, even if you take longer than that to finish the cycle. You owe it to yourselves to complete the entire plan at least once.

After you've completed it, you will be ready to experiment with the additional exercises in chapter 5, "Ecstasy Recipe—Your Joyous

Steps to Bliss" and chapter 6, "Continuing Your Practice."

We recommend that you don't add other activities from the book until you complete the full twenty-eight days, but that's not a rule. Experiment with everything in this manual to discover what works best for you. You might start with the first exercise from chapter 5 and systematically continue to the last exercise in chapter 6. Or you might pick and choose the ones that appeal most to try first. Either way, if something doesn't seem to work for you the first time, make sure you try it again later. As you gain knowledge, experience, and skill, many possibilities will appeal to you that did not attract or hold your attention at first.

The techniques we teach in this book are a distillation of over twenty years of sacred sex practice. For more than a decade, we've also been teaching others how to apply these methods to transform their relationship into a spiritual practice, to make ordinary sex into something sacred, and to continue to create love for a lifetime together. Everything in this book works, but not everything will suit every couple. Give yourself a year or more of practice before you put this book aside. By that time your love life will have been completely transformed, bringing you more happiness, joy and love than you ever dreamed possible.

Intercourse Positions for Circulating Sexual Energy

You've already been introduced to two of the most powerful energy exchange intercourse positions—the Yab Yum on Day 23 and the Lovers' Scissors on Day 28. Perhaps you've even experimented with these potent poses.

During the Yab Yum, you're sitting in a unified version of a standard meditation posture—your center of gravity is stable, your back is straight, your shoulders are relaxed, your mind is focused, everything's in its perfect place. With a little help from conscious breath, toned PC muscles, and a willing heart, you'll be able to direct your energy throughout your system. Begin with the small circuit, connecting genitals to hearts, as described during Week 4. When you've become attuned to the energy flow, you'll be able to guide it in many ecstatic variations. Experiment with these Yab Yum mixtures:

- The Genital-Mouth Loop: Enlarge your circuit to send the energy from his genitals, up her center to her mouth, out through her mouth on her breath, into his mouth, down the center of his body, and back to his genitals.

- The Figure Eight: Send the energy through other channels—up the spine and down the front of the body, rather than up the center. In the Figure Eight, on his exhale, he directs energy from his lingam into her yoni, she draws it in and directs it up her back to her crown, then down the front channel back to her yoni. On her exhale she directs the energy from her yoni into his lingam, he draws it in and directs it up his back to his crown, then down the front channel back to his lingam, and so on.

- The Reverse Figure Eight: On his exhale, he sends energy through his genitals into hers. She inhales, pulling the energy up the front of her body to her crown. She exhales, directing energy down the back channel to her yoni and out into his lingam. As he inhales, he draws the energy up his front channel to his crown, then down his spine, and so on.

- The Infinity Loop: Using harmonized breathing—inhaling and exhaling at the same time—with mouths together in a tender, open kiss, both lovers inhale through the nose, then give a PC squeeze and draw energy up their spines to their crowns. Exhaling through the mouth, they send energy out with their breath into one another and direct it down the partner's front channel to the genitals.

Although the Lovers' Scissors is easier on the body than the Yab Yum, it's a little more challenging to direct energy in particular pathways because you're lying down. At first, it's simpler to allow the energy to follow its own path as you concentrate on your genital, heart, and eye connection. However, with focused repetitions you'll also be able to make mystical magic with conscious energy circulation in this loving pose. Experiment with directing it through front, back, and center channels—without judgment or expectations.

Ten More Energy Exchange Poses

1. THE LEANING YAB YUM

In this more restful version of the Yab Yum, you sit facing each other. A firm mat or rug on the floor gives more support than a soft bed mattress. He stretches his legs out in front, opening them wide enough for her to snuggle in between. As she glides in close to him, lifting her legs over his, he slips his lingam tenderly into her yoni.

Connected in this loving way, both of you place your hands on the floor behind you, palms down, and lean your weight back on your arms. Making eye contact, settle into a harmonized breathing rhythm and begin PC squeezing. As you squeeze, visualize energy pulsing up the center of your body. In a brilliant beam, it flows out your crown chakra and joins with your lover's energy above your heads in the magnificent union of god and goddess.

2. THE HANDHOLDING POSITION

With the Yab Yum and the Lovers' Scissors you've primarily focused on sending energy up the front, back, and center of your body. But there are many more energy pathways throughout your system. The Handholding Position, another seated posture from the sixteenth-century Indian love manual the *Ananga Ranga,* works with "hot spots" in your hands and feet, creating a larger, more intricate circuit for energy flow. It requires some flexibility, especially for the woman and especially for holding this pose for any length of time.

He sits comfortably on a firm surface, and perhaps with some back support such as Liberator Shapes bedroom gear, or a meditation seat like the Back Jack. She slides down onto his lingam and sits in his lap. When they're nicely connected, he clasps her feet and holds onto them. She then reaches back to grasp and hold his feet. Try to match palms of hands to soles of feet, if you can. It's an enlivening and playful stance, because energy is released and spread by the very act of connecting this way.

3. FIXING A NAIL

A man-on-top position from the *Kama Sutra*, Fixing a Nail requires focus and flexibility. At first glance it appears unusual: our lady lover has the heel of her foot smack in the center of her man's forehead. But, as with all advice from the *Kama Sutra*, this pose has a purpose.

It's to awaken energy in the sixth chakra, the psychic, intuitive, mystical center.

To begin, she lies on her back with her legs stretched out. He kneels in front of her, his weight on his heels. She slides close and as he slips inside her, she lifts one leg and places her heel on his third eye, in the center of his forehead. With a slow and steady. pace, he thrusts rhythmically, and she matches the beat of his stroke with a light tap of her heel on his head. With each plunge, energy rides along from genitals to foot to head, inviting him to intuitive clarity. If he places a hand on the center of her chest, the fourth chakra, he'll broaden the circuit to bring in loving heart energy as well. If he places it on her third chakra, the solar plexus, as illustrated, energy directed there can help build her self-esteem.

4. PRESSED

Pressed, another *Kama Sutra* intercourse position, also involves using the feet as part of a conscious energy pathway. She's lying on her back with her knees drawn up tight to her chest. He kneels or squats in front of her and moves in very close for penetration. She then presses the soles of her feet firmly against his heart chakra, in the center of his chest between his nipples. She mirrors his thrust with a matching push of her legs in a sexy seesaw of sensual delight.

She visualizes delicious energy spreading from her yoni throughout her body, from head to toe. Where her feet meet his chest his heart opens to love and peace. He mixes this warmth with the fire from his groin for pure magic.

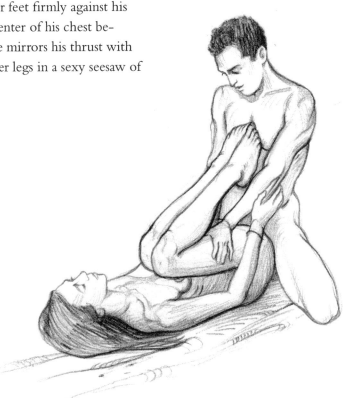

5. CLASPING SIDEWAYS

Yet another powerful posture from the *Kama Sutra*, Clasping Sideways is an amazing overall connector, marvelous for energy exchange in so many ways. Both of you lie on your sides—man on his left side, woman on her right—creating a special connection through your breath. Lying on one side opens the opposite air passage: a woman on her right side breathes through her left nostril, the feminine side of the energy system, while the man on his left side breathes through his right nostril, the masculine side of the energy system. Breathing together in a circular rhythm, you balance and harmonize your masculine and feminine energies.

When the partners are stretched out facing each other, penetration is fairly shallow. Your

bodies stay almost still; the only movement is an exquisitely slow rocking of your pelvis. With all your senses engaged and your mind acutely focused, Clasping Sideways is a marvelous position for encouraging the ecstatic wave of the Valley Orgasm, which grows from within and flows over and through you.

6. BELLY TO BELLY
(THE SEVENTEENTH MANNER)

Because they're hard to maintain for long, standing positions are usually best for quickies and building excitement, but because everything is upright they can also be powerful poses for an energy rush. Belly to Belly, from the fifteenth-century Arabian lovers' guide *The Perfumed Garden*, is one of the most user-friendly standing postures. As she stands facing him with her legs spread invitingly, he moves in for penetration with one foot slightly in front of the other. Holding each other close, you rock with the Bucket in the Well, a thrusting motion in which first he, then she, pushes the pelvis forward then pulls it back. You both keep your feet on the ground, but your energy rises to the heavens.

7. THE DEER

A sexy version of the Cat asana found in chapter 6, the Deer moves energy through her system in a rollicking wave. As she kneels down on all fours, he snuggles in behind her, grips her hips, and pulls her in tight for deep penetration. In time to his lingam lunges, she undulates her spine, sending a fire of intensity up through her body. Making sound helps draw the energy up even more.

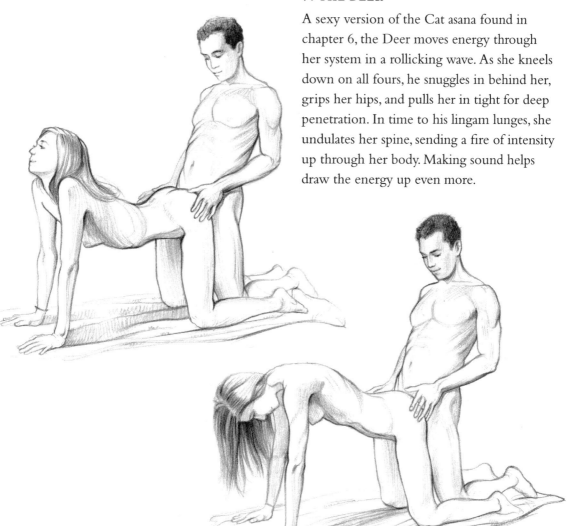

Consciously Circulating Energy for Health and Healing

During lovemaking you can consciously send energy to your partner to assist with physical and emotional healing. Because particular body positions direct energy to different parts of the body, lovers can make use of this phenomenon to help each other correct any imbalances and stay in all around tip-top shape.

In therapeutic lovemaking often only one partner moves, sending healing energy to the other, who lies still and quiet. The receptive partner calms the mind and focuses attention inside to guide the energy where it's needed for healing. Both the postures and the rhythm (sets of nine thrusts) are emphasized in the following positions to guide energy for particular types of healing.

8. RESTING THE SPIRIT AND HEALING YOUR SEXUAL ORGANS

You'll both get several benefits from this intercourse position—it invigorates your body, boosts low energy, calms a man's spirit, and helps keep a woman's reproductive system working well. She lies on her back, her legs

wide open, her upper body supported by a large pillow or a Liberator Shape like the Ramp. Lying atop her, he employs a thrusting pattern of three sets of nine. Particularly effective are deep-shallow thrusts, one deep one followed by eight shallow, all of them extremely slow and purposeful.

9. STRENGTHENING YOUR INTERNAL ORGANS

A slight variation on Clasping Sideways, this position brings health and vitality to all your internal organs. You both lie on your side. He keeps his legs stretched straight out, while she presses hers together and bends them back at the knees. This pose works equally well in either face-to-face or rear-entry versions. Experiment with both as you incorporate four sets of nine thrusts for maximum effect.

10. PAIR OF TONGS FOR INCREASING BLOOD COUNT

This woman-on-top position does wonders for your blood. She kneels or squats over him, legs spread wide enough to give him room to move, because although she's on top, he's the one giving the ride. She stays still, happily receiving his energetic gift. Using seven sets of nine thrusts will help correct menstrual irregularities, maintain stable blood pressure, increase blood count, and build overall strength.

Notes

1. Gabriel Pradiipaka is part of an Argentinean group hosting a website devoted to the exploration of non-dual Shaivism of Kashmir, including Tantra. This ritual is adapted from the one presented on the group's website. Pradiipaka does the translation from the original Sanskrit. http://www.sanskrit-sanscrito.com.ar/english/trika_tantricritual/tantricritual1.html#threecapeta.

2. *Upanishads—Mahanarayanopanisad*, section 65–66, http://www.hinduism.co.za/newpage4.htm.

3. *Chandamaharosana Tantra* (English), *Candamaharosana Tantra* (Sanskrit); *dPal gtum po khro bo chen po'i rgyud kyi rgyal po dpa'bo gcig pa* (Tibetan), ca. 700, http://www.yoniversum.nl/dakini/ttcanda.html, *The Candamaharosana Tantra* (Skt., Tib., and English), American Oriental Series, no. 56 (New Haven, CT: American Oriental Society, 1974). Although the exact time and origin of this Tantra are uncertain, the text is now being quoted more often, thanks to Christopher S. George's translation. It is recognized as one of the more important scriptures of Vajrayana Buddhism, the Tantric Buddhism of Tibet.

4. *Hevajra Tantra*, ca. 700, http://www.yoniversum.nl/dakini/tthevajra.html. This Buddhist Tantra of twenty chapters is thought to have originated in the eighth century. The male deity Hevajra personifies the Buddhist concept of a supreme being in the state of nonduality. As such he is most often depicted or visualized in sexual union (Tib., Yab Yum) with the goddess Nairatmya. Other sources include G. W. Farrow

and I. Menon, *The Concealed Essence of the Hevajra Tantra with the Commentary Yogaratnamala* (Delhi, 1992) and D. L. Snellgrove, *Hevajra Tantra: A Critical Study*, 2 vols. (London: Oxford University Press, 1959; reprinted 1980).

5. Miranda Shaw, *Passionate Enlightenment* (Princeton, NJ: Princeton University Press, 1994), 154.

6. *Kamakhya Tantra* as quoted by Chandra Alexandre, founder and executive director of SHARANYA, the Maa Batakali Cultural Mission.

7. Yoniversum is a wonderful website hosted by Rufus and Christina Camphausen. They present a wealth of information about Tantra, including a selection of ceremonial and ritual practices explained in great detail, including references back to the original Sanskrit.

> Home page: http://www.yoniversum .nl/central.html
> "Pancha Makara": http://www .yoniversum.nl/dakini/pancamak.html
> "Maithuna": http://www.yoniversum .nl/dakini/maithuna.html
> "Makara": http://www.yoniversum .nl/dakini/makara.html

8. Philip Rawson, *Art of Tantra* (New York: Thames & Hudson, 1985).

9. Gopi Krishna, "Tantric Sexual Rituals," http://www.mystae.com/restricted/ streams/scripts/tantra.html.

Recommended Reading and Resources

Breathing

Dennis Lewis, *Free Your Breath, Free Your Life: How Conscious Breathing Can Relieve Stress, Increase Vitality, and Help You Live More Fully* (ISBN: 1-590-30133-1). Lewis demonstrates how to find breathing practices most suitable to you—rather than assuming there is one best way for everyone to breathe. Choose from seven self-directed ways of working with breath. Want to reduce the stress load in your life? Breathing properly is one of the best places to start.

Dennis Lewis, *The Tao of Natural Breathing: For Health, Well-Being and Inner Growth* (ISBN: 0-965-16110-2). This book is an excellent guide on breathing for vitality, health, and spiritual awakening. It has been published in numerous languages.

Kama Sutra

AL LINK AND PALA COPELAND, *The Complete Idiot's Guide to Supercharged Kama Sutra* (ISBN: 978-1-5925-7574-9). At last: a book that really demystifies the ancient teachings of the original *Kama Sutra*. We offer detailed step-by-step instructions for kissing, touching, biting, slapping, sexual intercourse, cunnilingus, fellatio, intimate conversation, and using aphrodisiacs. This is a complete manual of sexual technique, gorgeously illustrated with full-color nude photos. Need we say, this is for connoisseurs of the art of love.

ALAIN DANIÉLOU, trans., *The Complete Kama Sutra,* by Vatsyayana (ISBN: 0-965-71782-8). Daniélou's translation is unabridged and includes the original numbering for all verses. Two complete commentaries appear with the relevant verses, with clear textual distinction. This is the best source for academic research and technical accuracy of translation. Unillustrated, this text is heavy reading.

INDRA SINHA, trans., *The Love Teachings of Kama Sutra: With Extracts from Koka Shastra, Ananga Ranga and Other Famous Indian Works on Love* (ISBN: 1-569-24779-X). Partially illustrated with photographs of Indian art and sculpture, Sinha's translation is more poetic than the Burton and Daniélou translations. He omits whole sections of the original text and takes considerable liberty in revising for accessibility to modern readers. He also includes passages from the *Ananga Ranga*. In both Burton's and Sinha's translations these passages are not clearly identified, making it difficult to separate the actual *Kama Sutra* text from the commentaries on it.

RICHARD FRANCIS BURTON AND F. F. ARBUTHNOT, trans., *The Kama Sutra of Vatsyayana.* Now in the public domain, Burton's 1883 translation is available on numerous websites. It also continues to be a top seller, with hundreds of editions published over the past century. Each edition typically has a newly authored introduction, and many are illustrated with line drawings or photographs, particularly featuring the sexual intercourse positions.

RICHARD FRANCIS BURTON AND F. F. AR-
BUTHNOT, trans., *Ananga Ranga (Stage of
the Bodiless One) or, The Hindu Art of Love
(Ars Amoris Indica)*. This 1885 translation,
too, is now in the public domain and
available on numerous websites. Also
from India, but much later than the *Kama
Sutra*, the *Ananga Ranga* is a manual of
love offering instruction to help couples
sustain a successful marriage by avoiding
some common pitfalls, particularly the
boredom that may result from lack of
sexual knowledge and skill. This book's
scope is no broader than the *Kama Sutra*'s,
and many consider it simply a summarizing
restatement.

RICHARD FRANCIS BURTON, trans., *The
Perfumed Garden of the Shaykh Nefwazi*.
Again, this translation (1886) is now in the
public domain and available on numerous
websites. *The Perfumed Garden* is the famous
Arabian love manual, written long after
both the *Kama Sutra* and the *Ananga Ranga*.
It goes beyond those two manuals only in
terms of style: a number of erotic, sensual,
sexy stories illustrate the teachings. A very
weak imitation of the *Kama Sutra*, at times

it is juvenile in its approach to sexuality, and
its tone is quite disparaging toward women.

JUDITH KURIANSKY, *The Complete Idiot's Guide
to Tantric Sex,* second edition (ISBN: 1-
592-57296-0). This 2004 edition has lots
of helpful information for beginners who
want to start introducing Tantric practices
into their busy lives. Kuriansky, a clinical
psychologist and sex therapist, is also a
certified Ipsalu Tantra teacher.

NICOLE BAILEY, *Pure Kama Sutra* (ISBN: 1-844-
83154-X). This is one of the best of the
illustrated versions of the *Kama Sutra*. Bailey
presents the sexual intercourse positions in
four categories: slow and soulful, fast and
passionate, deep and erotic, and adventurous.
She adds extra positions from the *Ananga
Ranga* and *The Perfumed Garden* and also
includes a chapter on Tantra.

NITYA LACROIX, *Kama Sutra: A Modern Guide to
the Ancient Art of Sex* (ISBN: 1-592-58038-
6). Lacroix is the author of more than forty
books on better sex, massage, Tantra, and the
Kama Sutra. This is one of the best illustrated
versions of the *Kama Sutra*. The intercourse

positions are particularly well presented and described, including a discussion of how they benefit men and women differently.

Richard Emerson, *Red-Hot Sex the Kama Sutra Way* (ISBN: 1-569-75463-2). This book is illustrated with lots of juicy color photos of couples showing the sexual intercourse positions and other love teachings from the *Kama Sutra*.

Taoist Sacred Sexuality— Books by Mantak Chia

The Multi-Orgasmic Woman: Discover Your Full Desire, Pleasure, and Vitality (ISBN: 1-594-86027-0). This book explores how women can adopt a pleasure orientation with sex rather than seeking orgasm as a goal of lovemaking. Nevertheless, it offers women a step-by-step guide to becoming multi-orgasmic.

The Multi-Orgasmic Man: Sexual Secrets Every Man Should Know (ISBN: 0-06251-336-2). This book is an excellent step-by-step how-to manual for achieving sexual ecstasy. In spite of the title, this book is for women as well as men.

The Multi-Orgasmic Couple (ISBN: 0-06251-614-0). Discover how to have multiple whole-body orgasms and reach ever more fulfilling levels of intimacy and ecstasy together.

Healing Love Through the Tao: Cultivating Female Sexual Energy (ISBN: 0-935-62105-9).

Taoist Secrets of Love: Cultivating Male Sexual Energy (ISBN: 0-943-35819-1). Mantak Chia is a master who gives detailed descriptions on the how-to of moving sexual energy. His methods are very disciplined and therefore work best for people who like structure and have patience and self-motivation. This book is also good for individuals not in relationship, because so much of the work is done on one's own. Because Chia's work derives from the Taoist tradition rather than the Tantric, there is more emphasis on the physical and practical than on the mystical and emotional aspects of the work. These books were among the most important to us as we cut our teeth on sacred sexuality.

Tantra

DANIEL COZORT, *Highest Yoga Tantra* (ISBN: 1-559-39036-0). This book explores the Tantric practices of generation and completion meditations leading to enlightenment. Emptiness and bliss are two of its main themes.

SHRI DHARMAKIRTI, *Mahayana Tantra: An Introduction* (ISBN: 0-143-02853-7). Shri Dharmakirti, practitioner of Mahayana Buddhist Tantra, is a disciple of the current Dalai Lama. He received initiations and instructions in the practice of highest secret mantra and was inducted into the lineage of Lama Tsongkhapa.

GEORG FEUERSTEIN, *Tantra: Path of Ecstasy* (ISBN: 1-570-62304-X). Feuerstein's work, drawn from Hindu sources, deals with the non-sexual aspects of Tantric practice. In the book he has assembled an important selection of Hindu, Tantric, and Shaivite texts difficult to find elsewhere.

KELSANG GYATSO GESHE, *Guide to Dakini Land: The Highest Yoga Tantra Practice of Buddha Vajrayogini* (ISBN: 0-948-00639-0).

A thorough explanation of the Tantric practice of Vajrayogini, the female Buddha of wisdom, this text provides detailed instructions on the eleven yogas of the generation stage and explains the essential completion stage practices leading to enlightenment. Also included are methods for transforming ordinary daily activities into spiritual meditations.

BHAGWAN SHREE RAJNEESH, *Tantra, the Supreme Understanding: Discourses on the Tantric Way of Tilopa's Song of Mahamudra* (ISBN: 0-880-50643-1). Unlike most Tantra authors, Bhagwan Rajneesh, also known as Osho, was undeniably a great Tantric master. This fact lends significant weight to his many publications on Tantra and sacred sexuality.

SWAMI SATYANANDA SARASWATI, *Kundalini Tantra* (ISBN: 8-185-78715-8). Swami Satyananda Saraswati founded the International Yoga Fellowship in 1963 and the Bihar School of Yoga in 1964. This text explores practices to awaken the kundalini energy.

SWAMI SATYANANDA SARASWATI, *Meditations from the Tantras* (ISBN: 8-185-78711-5). This book helps readers turn every action of life into an act of sadhana (spiritual practice) using meditation techniques with origins in Tantra.

PANDIT RAJMANI TIGUNAIT, *Sakti, the Power in Tantra: A Scholarly Approach* (ISBN: 0-893-89154-1). This book clarifies how Tantric philosophy and practice unify the concepts of yantra, mandala, mantra, chakra, kundalini, deities, and ritualistic and meditative practices. It explains the relationship among the various branches of Tantra and explores some of the controversy about the differences between right-hand (non-sexual) and left-hand (sexual) Tantric practices.

THE DALAI LAMA TSONG-KA-PA AND JEFFREY HOPKINS, *Deity Yoga: In Action and Performance Tantra* (ISBN: 0-937-93850-5). This book teaches the meditative techniques of Action and Performance Tantras.

THE DALAI LAMA TSONG-KA-PA AND JEFFREY HOPKINS, *Tantra in Tibet* (ISBN: 0-937-93849-1). Excellent discussion of the Tantric doctrine of emptiness.

WEI WU WEI, *Why Lazarus Laughed: The Essential Doctrine, Zen–Advaita–Tantra* (ISBN: 1-591-81011-6). Wei Wu Wei, who has become an underground cult figure, explores the essential doctrine shared by the traditions of Zen Buddhism, Advaita Vedanta, and Tantra. Born in Ireland in 1895 and raised in England, he attended Oxford and then traveled throughout Asia, spending some time at the ashram of Sri Ramana Maharshi. He published eight books before his death in 1986 at age 90.

DAVID GORDON WHITE, ed., *Tantra in Practice* (ISBN: 0-691-05778-8). This book includes plays, transcribed interviews, poetry, parodies, inscriptions, instructional texts, scriptures, philosophical conjectures, dreams, and astronomical speculations. These thirty-six texts from China, India, Japan, Nepal, and Tibet range from the seventh century to the present day.

LAMA YESHE, PHILIP GLASS, AND JONATHAN LANDAW, eds., *Introduction to Tantra: The Transformation of Desire* (ISBN: 0-861-71162-9). This is primarily a non-sexual exploration of Tantra. Al particularly likes the section on the subject of death and after death.

Tantra—Books by Daniel Odier

Daniel Odier, who has taught Eastern spiritual traditions at a number of American universities, founded the Tantra/Chan (Zen) Center in Paris. In addition to his books on Tantra, he has also published mystery novels, one of which was made into an award-winning film, *Devi the Goddess.* His novels are published under the pseudonym of Delacorta. Of all the Tantra books Al has read over the past twenty years, Odier's *Desire* and *Tantric Quest* are his top two choices.

Desire: The Tantric Path to Awakening (ISBN: 0-892-81858-1). According to Buddhism and to almost all the great world religions, desire is an enemy blocking the path to enlightenment. Contrary to this, Daniel Odier maintains that desire is the only true path to liberation, and the primary requirement for a spiritual seeker to fully awaken is simple, direct, personal experience. He refers to his disciplined approach as "micropractices" involving the conscious withdrawal from habitual activities for just a few seconds several times a day. There is no goal in this practice, no seeking to get somewhere or accomplish something, but rather the purpose is simply to be fully aware, fully awake, and fully present to your own divinity in the now moment. Odier describes his Tantric path as "nothing spectacular . . . lack[ing] in the exotic, the magickal, the extraordinary . . . there was no ritual other than to breathe, walk, bathe . . . to look at the earth, the lichens, the trees, the leaves, common objects; to enter deeply into contact with life, reality." He suggests that the "luminosity of existence" pervades everything, including you. Odier received direct personal Tantric initiation from a Kashmiri Shaivite yogini, Lalita Devi, in the Tantric lineage of the Tibetan master Kalu Rinpoche, which dates back several thousand years.

Yoga Spandakarika: The Sacred Texts at the Origins of Tantra (ISBN: 1-594-77051-4). This book presents translations of early Tantras (sacred Tantric texts).

Tantric Quest: An Encounter with Absolute Love (ISBN: 0-892-81620-1). In this story of his personal spiritual quest to find a Tantric master, Odier wanders through India where an unusual, and sometimes disastrous, sequence of events leads him deep in the forest to yogini Lalita Devi. Over a period of months, Odier undergoes a series of trials, tests, and rituals of purification that culminate in a sacred sex initiation in which he experiences the awakening of the kundalini and the joining of the divine forces of Shiva and Shakti.

Nirvana Tao: The Secret Meditation Techniques of the Taoist and Buddhist Masters (ISBN: 0-892-81045-9). Odier's teaching emphasizes direct personal experience to reach enlightenment, using visualization and meditation. Here he reveals secret spiritual practices of masters with whom he studied at Buddhist and Taoist monasteries throughout India, Nepal, Sri Lanka, Thailand, and Japan.

Tantric Sacred Sexuality

PALA COPELAND AND AL LINK, *Soul Sex: Tantra for Two* (ISBN: 1-564-14664-2) Our first book explores relationship as spiritual practice using Tantric and Taoist approaches to sacred sexuality. We help you learn how to create love for a lifetime together.

AL LINK AND PALA COPELAND, *Sensual Love Secrets for Couples: The Four Freedoms of Body, Mind, Heart & Soul* (ISBN: 978-0-7387-0965-9). In this book we explore the theme of relationship as spiritual practice. *Sensual Love Secrets* offers a relationship recipe with a difference. A practical, user-friendly guide for couples, it approaches life and relationships through the essential elements of human nature—your body, mind, heart, and soul—your four freedoms. Includes more than 100 simple and playful exercises.

MARGO ANAND, *The Art of Sexual Ecstasy: The Path of Sacred Sexuality for Western Lovers* (ISBN: 0-874-77581-7). This book is a complete sacred sex course in itself. With lots of meditations, activities, and exercises, it is particularly suited for couples who want to open up to each other emotionally as well as physically.

NIK DOUGLAS AND PENNY SLINGER, *Sexual Secrets: The Alchemy of Ecstasy* (ISBN: 0-892-81805-0). First published in 1979, this popular book (over 1 million copies sold) presents a concise and articulate overview of the history and philosophy of sacred sex. Practical exercises and meditations are interspersed throughout. It's suited for people who seek background knowledge, and who like to pick, choose, and create the activities for their own exploration. It overflows with Slinger's wonderful erotic drawings.

JULIE HENDERSON, *The Lover Within: Opening to Energy in Sexual Practice* (ISBN: 1-581-77017-0). This book is an excellent how-to manual for working with your sexual energy. It might alter both how you think about love and sex and what you do in intimate practice. The author provides exercises to be experienced alone or with a partner and offers instruction on how to move, collect, heighten, and share energy.

DIANA RICHARDSON, *Tantric Orgasm for Women* (ISBN: 0-892-81133-1). This book is an excellent presentation of information about the polarity of the various chakras and the role of breasts in the female orgasmic response. It contains the best discussion we have seen of the experience of a valley orgasm: the author explains how to relax into a whole-body orgasm rather than achieving it as a goal.

MA ANANDA SARITA AND SWAMI ANAND GEHO, *Ecstatic Sex: A Guide to the Pleasures of Tantra* (ISBN: 0-743-24610-1). This text explores Tantric sexuality, including basic sexual anatomy, opening the chakras, self-pleasuring, foreplay, creative positions, and orgasm. Ma Ananda Sarita and Swami Anand Geho have taught Tantra at Osho Multiversity in India.

MA ANANDA SARITA AND SWAMI ANAND GEHO, *Tantric Love: A Nine Step Guide to Transforming Lovers into Soul Mates* (ISBN: 0-743-21531-1). This book illustrates ways couples can open to a deeper intimacy. Each chapter focuses on one of the chakras and offers simple exercises to help you share this energy, opening the door to ecstasy.

Audio & Video

ANAL SEX AND PROSTATE MASSAGE DVDs (Order from http://www.tantra-sex.com/v-anal.html). Here are three excellent video productions from Joseph Kramer and the EROSpirit Research Institute. Highly informative for heterosexuals as well as gays, all three DVDs offer techniques and information about anatomy, hygiene, healing, and giving pleasure.

- *Gay Sex Wisdom Vol. 9: Rosebud Massage*
- *Gay Sex Wisdom Vol. 10: Exploring the Land Down Under*
- *Uranus: Self Anal Massage for Men*

TANTRA.COM, *Ancient Secrets of Sexual Ecstasy* DVD (Order from http://www.tantra-sex.com/v-tantra.html). This is by far the best video available on sacred sexuality for modern lovers. We recommend only the X-rated version, whose explicit sequences are erotic, informative, and artfully presented. It is packed with useful techniques lovers can apply immediately.

PALA COPELAND AND JEFF DAVIES, *Apertio: Tantra Energy Meditations* CD (ASIN: B000054490) (Order from http://www.tantra-sex.com). Pala Copeland guides you through energy meditations set to the mystical music of Jeff Davies. Learn to feel your energy body—calm it, balance it, play with it—and join it with your beloved.

DEBORAH SUNDAHL, FEMALE EJACULATION INSTRUCTIONAL DVDs (Order from http://www.tantra-sex.com/v-female.html). Titles include *How to Female Ejaculate, Tantric Journey to Female Orgasm,* and *Female Ejaculation for Couples.*

JULI ASHTON SEX GUIDE DVDs (Order from http://www.tantra-sex.com/v-juli.html). Titles include *Swinging: From Fantasy to Reality, Toys for Great Sex, Erotic Seduction: Dressing and Undressing for Great Sex,* and *Sex Around the House.*

KAMA SUTRA SEXUAL POSITIONS DVDs (Order from http://www.tantra-sex.com/v-kama.html). A selection of videos guiding couples in their exploration of the many sexual intercourse positions mentioned in the *Kama Sutra,* the *Ananga Ranga,* and *The Perfumed Garden.*

NINA HARTLEY SEX GUIDE DVDs (Order from http://www.tantra-sex.com/v-ninaguides .html). Titles include *Making Love to Women, Guide to Sex Toys, Guide to Anal Sex, Guide to Private Dancing, Guide to Seduction, Guide to Foreplay, Guide to Alternative Sex, Guide to Swinging, Guide to Oral Sex,* and *Guide to Cunnilingus.*

RICHARD AND DIANA DAFFNER, *Tantra Tai Chi for Couples* (ASIN: 0967290007). Directors Richard and Diana Daffner are certified instructors of Tai Chi Chih. Diana holds a black belt in Aikido. They present a sequence of qigong-style exercises for couples, exercises that stimulate sexual energy and support spiritual awakening, all within the context of a loving relationship.

Internet Sources

AL LINK AND PALA COPELAND, *100 Ways to Keep Your Lover* (eBook) (Order from http://www.tantra-sex.com/100Ways .html). With this proactive and interactive eBook, everything you need to live the good life—a sensual, sexy, romantic life—is only a click away. It is proactive in that we encourage you to take positive action to put love, passion, and romance at the center of your life together. We have distilled the essence of nurturing relationship, keeping monogamy hot, and sustaining passionate romance into 100 sexy activities you can implement immediately. We tell you exactly what to do. These ideas and activities are quite simple, yet imaginative and daring.

4 FREEDOMS RELATIONSHIP TANTRA (http:// www.tantra-sex.com) (Contact by email: 4freedoms@tantraloving.com). Sacred sexuality weekends are held monthly near Ottawa, Canada, facilitated by Al Link and Pala Copeland. The site offers a large selection of pro-sexual learning resources including books, music, videos, and sensual products. with many links to free articles and other sexuality websites.

4 Freedoms Guide to Aphrodisiacs (http://www.tantra-sex.com/aphrodisiacs.html). Our free online guide to aphrodisiacs for men and women includes detailed reviews of many aphrodisiac products and formulas with links to Internet suppliers.

4 Freedoms Guide to Pheromones (http://www.tantra-sex.com/ep6.html#lure). If you want to experiment with pheromones, here is our online guide to some of the best available on the Internet, with links to suppliers.

4 Freedoms Guide to Sex Toys (http://www.tantra-sex.com/sextoyprimer.html). Our online guide to sex toys includes links to suppliers on the Internet.

4 Freedoms Guide to Music for Lovers (http://www.tantra-sex.com/erotic-music.html). This is our online music store with links to some of the CDs we find sexy and romantic.

Pala Copeland and Al Link, *Awakening Women's Orgasm* (eBook) (Order from http://www.tantra-sex.com/womenorgasm.html). Women have a capacity for orgasm that is truly awesome. It is a power of pleasure that ranges from sweet to sublime to superlative and it is one that almost every woman can unleash, simply by learning a few new things and unlearning a few old ones. In this eBook you will learn about the many different types of orgasm a woman's body is waiting to give her, and about the emotional and energetic experience of sex. Exercises for mind, heart, and body help women open up to their sexual selves, on their own and with their partners.

4 Freedoms Link to Classic Texts. The full Burton translations of the *Ananga Ranga* (1885), the *Kama Sutra* (1883), and *The Perfumed Garden* (1886) are available free at our website:

- http://www.tantra-sex.com/anangaranga.html
- http://www.tantra-sex.com/kamasutra.html
- http://www.tantra-sex.com/perfumedgarden.html

INTERNET SACRED TEXT ARCHIVE (http://www.sacred-texts.com/index.htm). This searchable database contains sacred, spiritual, and religious texts from around the world and for all faiths. Many are presented in full, as they are now in the public domain. Here you will find the complete texts for the Burton translations of the *Kama Sutra*, the *Ananga Ranga* and *The Perfumed Garden*.

KAMA SUTRA OILS OF LOVE® (Order from http://www.tantra-sex.com/ep6.html #lotions). A fine selection of sensual massage oils. Note: these products actually have nothing to do with the *Kama Sutra*; the name is merely used as a marketing strategy to gain attention and consumer confidence.

LIBERATOR® SHAPES—BEDROOM ADVENTURE GEAR (Order from http://www.tantra-sex.com/liberatorshapes.html). This gear can help you experiment with all the intercourse positions in the *Kama Sutra*, and do so in comfort and style. The foam cores covered in washable fabrics are stackable for creative combinations to enhance your lovemaking.

MINKGLOVE.COM—HANDMADE FUR MASSAGE GLOVES (http://tantra-sex.com/recommends/MinkgLove). Choose from genuine rabbit, fox, chinchilla, and mink fur. The feeling of these gloves against your skin is pure pleasure and delight. This is one of the sexiest products we have seen in a long time.

AL LINK AND PALA COPELAND, *Tantra and Kama Sutra Sex Positions* (eBook) (Order from http://www.tantra-sex.com/KamaSutraPositions.html). Expand your lovemaking repertoire and increase your pleasure with this photo manual of Tantra and Kama Sutra sex positions. In this modern interpretation of classic love postures, full-page color photos capture the emotional and energetic connection of sacred lovemaking as they illustrate positions and techniques. Each photo is accompanied by comments on how and why the position is used. We also include useful information about sacred sex practices.

TANTRA.COM (http://www.tantra.com). Tantra.com maintains a database of sacred sexuality teachers and workshops around the planet, but only including those websites that pay for a listing. Tantra.com produced the excellent sacred sexuality instruction DVD *Ancient Secrets of Sexual Ecstasy.*

TANTRIC SEX PARTNERS (http://www.tantra-sex.com/ep11.html#personals). Find a Tantric sex partner, or perhaps your soul mate. A number of couples attending our sacred relationship weekends found each other on the Internet.

AL LINK AND PALA COPELAND, *Voluntary Ejaculation and Male Multiple Orgasms* (eBook) (Order from http://www.tantra-sex.com/EjaculationMastery.html). Learn simple techniques to master your ejaculation response, making it completely voluntary. Ejaculate when and if you want to. Take your lovemaking to unimagined new heights with the easy-to-learn techniques taught in this eBook.

About the Authors

Al Link and Pala Copeland have been leading retreats on sacred loving for ten years. As experts on the subject of sexuality and Tantra, they have appeared on radio and television and have been featured in many publications, such as *Ladies' Home Journal, Redbook, Body & Soul,* and the *Wall Street Journal.* They are the authors of three previous books: *Soul Sex: Tantra for Two, The Complete Idiot's Guide to Supercharged Kama Sutra,* and *Sensual Love Secrets for Couples: The Four Freedoms of Body, Mind, Heart & Soul.* They live in Ottawa, Canada. Visit their website at www.tantra-sex.com.

To Write to the Authors

If you wish to contact the authors or would like more information about this book, please write to the authors in care of Llewellyn Worldwide and we will forward your request. Both the authors and publisher appreciate hearing from you and learning of your enjoyment of this book and how it has helped you. Llewellyn Worldwide cannot guarantee that every letter written to the authors can be answered, but all will be forwarded. Please write to:

Pala Copeland & Al Link
℅ Llewellyn Worldwide
2143 Wooddale Drive, Dept. 978-0-7387-0999-4
Woodbury, MN 55125-2989, U.S.A.

Please enclose a self-addressed stamped envelope for reply,
or $1.00 to cover costs. If outside U.S.A., enclose
international postal reply coupon.

Many of Llewellyn's authors have websites with additional information and resources. For more information, please visit our website at:

www.llewellyn.com